Israel's Final Holocaust

Israel's Final Holocaust

Dr. Jack Van Impe
and
Roger F. Campbell

Jack Van Impe Ministries
Box 7004 · Troy, Michigan 48007

In Canada:
Box 1717 · Postal Station A · Windsor, Ontario N9A 6Y1

www.jvim.com

ISBN#0-934803-08-0

Copyright © 1979 by Jack Van Impe Crusades

Printed in the United States of America.

Seventeenth Printing, 2015.

Jack Van Impe Ministries
P.O. Box 7004
Troy, Michigan 48007-7004

In Canada:
P.O. Box 1717, Postal Station A
Windsor, Ontario N9A 6Y1

www.jvim.com

ISBN# 0-934803-08-0

To Reverend Oscar Van Impe, my father, whose diligent study and memorization of the Scriptures shaped my ministry and whose prayers undergrid our worldwide work.

Dr. Jack Van Impe

To Reverend Martin Blok, my father-in-law, who first gave me an opportunity to preach.

Roger F. Campbell

CONTENTS

INTRODUCTION

World conditions, especially the tense Middle East situation, have aroused interest in Bible prophecy to an all-time high. But it is impossible to grasp God's prophetic plan apart from an understanding of His promises to Israel.

All prophetic truth revolves around the Jews. The Bible reviews their history and unfolds their future. The future of the world will be affected by the future of Israel.

In this work we will give special attention to the dispersion and sufferings of the Jewish people, believing this will lead to a better understanding between Jews and Gentiles and that it will help readers to appreciate the Jewish longing for a national home.

The history of the Jews during the past two thousand years is a panorama of persecution. It is doubtful that any people have suffered so consistently and so long as have the descendents of Abraham, Isaac, and Jacob.

Anti-Semitism is a cancer that never seems to heal. Although there have been periods of respite, this evil has erupted periodically, bringing misery and heartache to the children of Israel.

Are we about to witness another wave of persecution of Jews?

Old Testament prophets were careful to outline the events of the end time as they would affect Israel and the world. They saw a return of the Jews to their homeland in the latter days. Does the existence of the State of Israel fulfill that prophecy?

Today, most Christians are acquainted with terms in the prophecy vocabulary, such as the Rapture of the church, the Tribulation period, the Antichrist, the mark of the Beast, Armageddon, and the Millennium. What do these mean? And when will the events of which they speak find fulfillment?

We present this work as an aid in understanding Bible prophecy as it relates to Israel and the world. These pages will reveal the source of peace in troubled times.

Dr. Jack Van Impe
Roger F. Campbell

Israel's
Final
Holocaust

1
ALL THE WORLD'S A STAGE

In 1860, a French scientist named Pierre Berchelt predicted: "Within a hundred years of physical and chemical science, man will know what the atom is. It is my belief that when science reaches this stage, God will come down with His big ring of keys and will say to humanity: 'Gentlemen, it is closing time.' " [1]

The first part of Berchelt's forecast is history. We live in the perilous atomic age. But what about the remainder of the prediction? How near is closing time?

And what is closing?

Are we to expect the end of the world? Judgment? Will some power-hungry leader plunge the world into a life ending nuclear nightmare? Will experiments in germ warfare or the creation of new life forms bring about scientific suicide?

Today's uncertainties have produced immense interest in the future. Something is in the wind, and it has not gone unnoticed. Mystics, psychics, and leaders of occult groups have seized this opportunity to swell the ranks of their followers. Astrology is flourishing; instruction for living in tune with the stars is available in nearly every newspaper. False prophets are legion and their very presence in ever-increasing numbers is a fulfillment of prophecy.

But curiosity about the future is not new. Even the disciples longed for more light on things to come when they asked, "...*what shall be the sign of thy coming, and of the end of the world*?" (Matt. 24:3).

The Lord's answer to their question, along with other Bible prophecies, provides a composite of required conditions for closing time.

War

And ye shall hear of wars and rumors of wars: see that ye be not troubled: for all these things must come to pass, but the end is not yet. For nation shall rise against nation, and kingdom against kingdom... (Matt. 24:6, 7).

War seems unthinkable in this era of unparalleled education. One would think that enlightened man would have forsaken such a barbaric practice. Yet the twentieth century, more than any other, has demonstrated that full heads and empty hearts produce violence. Twice in the span of a generation, Europe's most scientifically advanced nation plunged the world into bloody conflict.

William Howard Taft wrote: "The battlefield as a place of settlement of disputes is gradually yielding to the arbitral courts of justice. The interests of great masses are not being sacrificed as in former times to the selfishness, ambitions, and aggrandizement of the sovereigns." [2]

Sounds like progress, doesn't it? But Mr. Taft wrote his evaluation in 1911.

Many years later, General Douglas MacArthur declared:

"Military alliances, balances of power, leagues of nations, all in turn failed, leaving the only path to be by way of the crucible of war. The utter destructiveness of war now blots out this alternative. We have had our last chance. If we will not devise some greater and more equitable system, Armageddon will be at the door. The problem basically is theological and involves a spiritual recrudescence and improvement of human character that will synchronize with our almost matchless advances in science, art, literature

14

and all material and cultural developments of the past 2,000 years. It must be of the spirit if we are to save the flesh." [3]

But the search for a more equitable system has been fruitless. Too many have died in battle since MacArthur's thought-provoking analysis. Genuine spiritual revival still has not taken place. The present worldwide military buildup surpasses any ever known.

And Armageddon approaches.

Although wars have been fought throughout history, the Bible says the end-time battles will be more frequent and disastrous. The situation is compared to a woman in travail—labor. The pains increase with frequency and severity as the birth draws near (Rom. 8:22,23).

Fifty-two million were killed in World War II, compared to eight million in World War I. The prospect of casualties in a future conflict is mind-boggling. Add to this the lingering effects of radiation poisoning and other damage, and Dr. David Bradley's conclusion in his book No Place to Hide is understandable. He wrote, "When one considers that one millionth of a gram of radium contained in the body may be fatal, one is inclined to turn from calculus to Christianity." [4]

Even small nations are assembling arsenals of doomsday proportions. This is another fulfillment of prophecy: "*Proclaim ye this among the Gentiles; Prepare war, wake up the mighty men, let all the men of war draw near; let them come up: beat your plowshares into swords, and your pruning hooks into spears: let the weak* [small nations] *say, I am strong*" (Joel 3:9,10).

Meanwhile, peace continues to be an elusive dream, as it has through the centuries. Though peace talks continue and disarmament dialogues claim spasmodic progress, tranquility will be temporary at best. "*For when they shall say, Peace and safety; then sudden destruction cometh upon them, as travail upon a woman with child; and they shall not escape*" (1 Thess. 5:3).

Famines, Pestilences, Earthquakes

...and there shall be famines, and pestilences, and earthquakes, in divers places (Matt. 24:7).

While living in a land of plenty it is difficult to envision widespread hunger. Yet famine is a way of life for a great part of the world. More than two billion people go to bed hungry every night.

About 10,000 people die daily because of a lack of food and the effects of malnutrition, but this will increase dramatically because of a multiplying world population. Although population growth has slowed in the United States, other parts of the world are increasing so fast that experts are unable to come up with an answer to the problem.

A few prominent people are advocating the "lifeboat" solution. This approach sees the ever-increasing number of people as impossible to feed, and foresees a day when dividing food among so many would mean the death of the entire race. The idea is to keep plenty of food in the productive areas—the lifeboats—and let the rest of the world starve.

The "lifeboat" solution view is held by a few Americans who undoubtedly see our land as one of the lifeboats. But even our food sufficiency hangs by a very thin thread.

What if God should withhold rain from America for even one year? What if storms or plant diseases ruined our bountiful harvests? What if tractors sat idle in the fields because energy could not be bought to run them? Our surplus would then be but memories. As in Pharaoh's dream, the lean years would soon devour the fat ones. Hunger would stalk the fruited plains. And the "lifeboat" solution would be the farthest option from our minds.

Pestilence frequently accompanies famine. Often it may be the cause of it. The insect world is multiplying at an unbelievable rate. Entomologists estimate the number has now climbed to one

16

quintillion, including five million different species. The weight of all the insects in the world would be twelve times the combined weight of the entire human race. The insect problem is compounded by the ability of many varieties to develop immunities to our most powerful pesticides.

Many top scholars identify the biblical term "pestilence" with cancer. A number of dictionaries, as well as the *Amplified New Testament*, define it as "malignancy, malignant growths, or cancer." It is well known that exposure to radiation causes malignancies. Nuclear war may well be the cause of much of the pestilence of the last days.

Experiments in germ warfare or in the development of new life forms may bring pestilence. Safety measures have failed to protect the public on some occasions and many people are concerned about the possibility of a laboratory accident or some freak development in an experiment that could bring a plague of major proportions for which there is no known cure.

Earthquakes are taking place on an unprecedented scale. The United States Geodetic Service reports one million earthquakes annually. Often as many as twenty tremors are in progress simultaneously.

Seismologists inform us that the North Pole is tilted off center. This is expected to bring about the most devastating earthquakes in history. Biblical prophecies are unfailing, and in God's time an unprecedented earthquake epidemic is certain. The greatest quake is yet to come; it will take place when Christ returns to earth.

> *And his feet shall stand in that day upon the mount of Olives, which is before Jerusalem on the east, and the mount of Olives shall cleave in the midst thereof toward the east and toward the west, and there shall be a very great valley; and half of the mountain shall remove toward the north, and half of it toward the south* (Zech. 14:4).

Sliding Morals

And because iniquity shall abound, the love of many shall wax cold (Matt. 24:12).

A lady once prayed, "Lord forgive me! I do so many things that I used to think were wrong."

Her prayer could be prayed by millions. The sexual revolution is now history and its bitter effects remain. Fornication, adultery, and even homosexuality have gained respectability. Nevertheless, neither new and more appealing names nor a change in public opinion have altered the seriousness of these practices in the mind of God. "Premarital relationships," "affairs," and "gays" may be words designed to take the shame out of old labels, but the wages of sin remain the same.

We are told that media productions reflect the state of public taste and morality. If that is true, the days of Noah are upon us.

Television has been called a vast wasteland. That may be too complimentary. Writers purporting to create realism have made the tube a dumping ground for their pitiful products. Even families who are careful about their language have dropped barriers and allowed television characters to profane their homes. Burlesque shows and striptease acts have moved from night clubs to living rooms. Prostitution and homosexuality are often portrayed favorably before the whole family.

Shades of Sodom! And all to sell merchandise.

Ironically, we are becoming more puritanical about our environment but not about our lives. We say we want clean air, clean water, and clean countryside's. But what good is a clean environment filled with polluted bodies and minds?

Increased Knowledge

But thou, O Daniel, shut up the words, and seal the book, even to the time of the end: many shall run to and fro, and knowl-

edge shall be increased (Dan. 12:4).

For centuries the world seemed to slumber. Thousands of years passed without major changes in most areas of life. Paul and Columbus sailed in similar ships even though their voyages were nearly fifteen hundred years apart. Medical know-how moved at a snail's pace.

Then came an explosion of knowledge, a rash of life changing discoveries and inventions. People who had traveled in horse-drawn vehicles lived to see the skies filled with jet planes and men walking on the moon. The atom was split, ushering in the nuclear age with its perils and possibilities. Miracle drugs that conquered old killer diseases were discovered and vaccines were developed that eliminated former plague producers.

Now we are in the age of computers. These electronic minds are entering every area of life. Former methods of office proce-dures have been made obsolete. The fact that records on millions of people are available at the push of the proper buttons is a dis-turbing thought if wicked men come into power.

Computers seem almost human. They have memories. They solve difficult problems. They even speak. Computers will undoubtedly be employed by the prophesied final world dictator in his move to control people and the economies of the world. These space-age wonders will make it possible to enforce the receiving of a special mark in the hand or forehead that, in a future day, will be required in order to buy or sell merchandise. Starvation and martyrdom will be the lot of any who refuse this beastly identifica-tion. (More about this mysterious mark later.)

Each day seems to unveil some invention that baffles most of us.

What does the knowledge explosion mean?
Why did this breakthrough tarry for so long?
Why was it reserved for closing time?

The Rabbis Speak

For decades, certain Orthodox rabbis have maintained that the Messiah would come when three signs were in evidence at the same time.

First, there must be speeding chariots in the streets of Jerusalem, fulfilling Nahum 2:4: *"The chariots shall rage in the streets, they shall jostle one against another in the broad ways: they shall seem like torches, they shall run like the lightnings."*

This interesting verse once prompted Sir Isaac Newton to predict that men would someday travel as fast as forty miles per hour.

Voltaire, an enemy of Christianity in that era, scorned Newton's statement, saying, "See what a fool Christianity makes of an otherwise brilliant man, such as Sir Isaac Newton! Doesn't he know that if a man traveled forty miles an hour, he would suffocate and his heart would stop?"

But Newton was conservatively correct. And today, in Jerusalem, as in other major cities, speeding chariots (automobiles) jostle one against another in the broad ways. At night they seem like torches and they run like lightning.

The second sign, the rabbis said, would be the protection of Jerusalem by men flying as birds. *"As birds flying, so will the Lord of hosts defend Jerusalem; defending also he will deliver it; and passing over he will preserve it"* (Isa. 31:5).

No wonder Israelis are convinced they must retain air superiority in the Middle East. Already the accomplishments of their top-notch pilots are almost legendary. Jets over Jerusalem have more significance than in any other place on earth. And the sky over that city is seldom silent.

The third requirement of the rabbis was the blossoming of the desert. *"The wilderness and the solitary place shall be glad for them; and the desert shall rejoice, and blossom as the rose"* (Isa. 35:1).

Although the complete fulfillment of this promise is for a better day yet to come, the desert is blossoming in Israel. Near miracles have been performed in an area that once was barren and waste. The agricultural successes of the Jews in the final days are foretold in a number of prophetic Scriptures, some of which we will explore later.

The Messiah of Israel, the Savior of the world, has already come, but His return is signaled by numerous signs, including those proclaimed by the waiting rabbis.

Signs in the Heavens

"And there shall be signs in the sun, and in the moon, and in the stars; and upon the earth distress of nations, with perplexity; the sea and the waves roaring" (Luke 21:25).

For all who have watched humans walking, driving, and planting a flag on the moon, this prophecy needs no explanation. Had someone predicted this at the turn of the century, he might have been placed under psychiatric treatment. But it has happened in our generation.

Christ also spoke of startling calamities in space. After discussing signs in the sun, moon, and stars, He said: *"Men's hearts [shall be] failing them for fear, and for looking after those things which are coming on the earth: for the powers of heaven shall be shaken"* (Luke 21:26).

Although he counts himself progressive and civilized, man still employs the best minds on earth to search constantly for more deadly weapons. After the bombing of Hiroshima, Charles Lindbergh lamented: "Hiroshima was as far from the intention of the pure scientist as the Inquisition was from the Sermon on the Mount." [5] Nevertheless, the drive for more potent killers continues and their area of operation has now reached the heavens, another indication that closing time is near.

The World Stage

Perhaps most interesting in the study of future things is the fulfillment of prophecy concerning the movements of nations in the end time. On the world stage, closing scenes are being enacted.

The European Union, or Revived Roman Empire is growing in size and global reach. For generations, Bible scholars have been awaiting this international coalition, from which they expect a leader to rise who will guarantee peace in the Middle East, especially to Israel.

China is able to field an army of two hundred million men. Napoleon said of China, "There lies a sleeping giant. If he ever wakes he will shake the world. Let him sleep." But the giant is awake! Will Napoleon's prediction come true?

Finally, Israel is back in her land. This is the keystone of all Bible prophecy concerning the end time. All other factors of the prophetic picture would be meaningless had not the Jews returned to the land of their fathers.

Although the history of her people is a story of incredible difficulties, Israel's most trying times are ahead. We will review those awful sufferings of the past and preview the unparalleled trials that await Israel in the future.

The world scene all of history has been moving toward is upon us. We are not confronted with a few facts manipulated by a self-seeking prophet in an effort to gain followers. Instead, we are witnessing an unfolding of divinely designed circumstances that encompass the entire earth and its inhabitants.

The stage is set for closing time, and all the world is the stage.

2
PREVIEW

Skeptics dislike the prophet Daniel. His outline of the future is too accurate.

Taken captive in his teens by Nebuchadnezzar, king of Babylon, this young Hebrew was chosen to be one of the king's advisors. The king chose well; Daniel would become the most valuable man in the kingdom.

Nebuchadnezzar, powerful king of the Babylonian Empire, conquered Jerusalem and carried away the people of Judah for a captivity of seventy years. He rebuilt Babylon after its former decline and transformed it into one of the most unusual and beautiful cities of history.

Babylon covered an area of two hundred square miles and was surrounded by walls wide enough at the top to have rows of small houses with a space between them for the passage of chariots. There were fifty temples in the city as well as a huge complex of impressive buildings. The palace was built of blue enameled bricks; its construction carried the mark of master craftsmen, many of whom were probably captives chosen for this special project because of their abilities.

Here, too, Nebuchadnezzar built the famous hanging gardens as a special gift to his wife, a Median princess. They consisted of terraces, supported by massive masonry arches, on which carefully tended gardens had been laid out on different levels. These gardens contained a variety of Persian and Babylonian plants and trees. Vegetation transplanted from the queen's mountain home was intended to comfort her when she was homesick. The Greeks considered the hanging gardens one of the Seven Wonders of the World.

Into this beauty and splendor, four young Hebrew men were brought to become members of the king's staff of advisors, or wise men. Among them was Daniel the prophet.

Not long after arriving in Babylon, Daniel and his three friends found themselves in serious trouble. An order went out from the king to execute all the wise men, due to their inability to interpret a dream that had come to Nebuchadnezzar. They might have been able to bluff their way through an interpretation, but the king could not even remember his dream, and so he had required that they tell him both the dream and the interpretation.

Stumped, they had grumbled: *"There is not a man upon the earth that can shew the king's matter: therefore there is no king, lord, nor ruler, that asked such things at any magician, or astrologer, or Chaldean"* (Dan. 2:10).

The king's reaction? Fury! *"For this cause the king was angry and very furious, and commanded to destroy all the wise men of Babylon. And the decree went forth that the wise men should be slain; and they sought Daniel and his fellows to be slain"* (Dan. 2:12, 13).

Upon receiving word of the order for execution, Daniel asked for time to pray and guaranteed that he would reveal the king's dream and its interpretation. In fulfilling that promise, Daniel gave us what has come to be known as the "ABC of Prophecy." Commenting on Nebuchadnezzar's dream and Daniel's interpretation, the late Dr. H. A. Ironside wrote: "I suppose it contains the most complete, and yet the most simple prophetic picture that we have in all the word of God." [1]

Nebuchadnezzar's Dream

Why did God give a preview of the future to a Gentile king

who had taken the Jews captive? We do not know. But that he did so is without question. History has proved the accuracy of that assessment. Fulfillment of the greater part of the preview has already taken place, and the stage is set for the remainder to develop. Pointing out the relevance of the king's dream to those who live near "closing time," Daniel said: "*But there is a God in heaven that revealeth secrets, and maketh known to the king Nebuchadnezzar what shall be in the latter days...*" (Dan. 2:28).

He then explained the dream and its interpretation:

"Thou, O King, sawest, and behold a great image. This great image, whose brightness was excellent, stood before thee; and the form thereof was terrible. This image's head was of fine gold, his breast and his arms of silver, his belly and his thighs of brass, His legs of iron, his feet part of iron and part of clay. Thou sawest till that a stone was cut out without hands, which smote the image upon his feet that were of iron and clay, and brake them to pieces. Then was the iron, the clay, the brass, the silver, and the gold, broken to pieces together, and became like the chaff of the summer threshingfloors; and the wind carried them away, that no place was found for them: and the stone that smote the image became a great mountain, and filled the whole earth" (Dan. 2:31-35).

The dream was of an image of a man with a head of gold, breast and arms of silver, midsection and thighs of brass, legs of iron, and feet that were part iron and part clay. The interpretation was simple and yet profound, easy to understand but veiled without Daniel's explanation. It is understood now by those who know the history of the rise and fall of Gentile empires from that day to this, and it is intriguing in its implications for the end time.

The head of gold represented Nebuchadnezzar, whose power in the Babylonian Empire was absolute. He must have listened with satisfaction to this part of the interpretation of his dream.

The breast and arms of the image represented the empire that would rise after the fall of Babylon, the Medo-Persian Empire. Though this kingdom was larger, the Medo-Persian leaders were less powerful than Nebuchadnezzar, since laws were enacted that limited rulers' decrees.

The third kingdom, represented by the belly and thighs of brass, was the Grecian Empire, headed by Alexander the Great.

The legs of iron symbolized the Roman Empire. The feet of the image, part iron and part clay, spoke of the revival of the Roman Empire in the last days, with the ten toes representing ten leaders of that coming European federation.

The great stone cut out of the mountain that fell on the feet of the image and destroyed it represents the coming kingdom of Christ that will be established upon His return to earth. Note that He will come when the final stage of the image is developed. If it can be shown that we are now at that point in history, there can be no doubt that closing time is near. The prophet Daniel was definite:

> *And in the days of these kings shall the God of heaven set up a kingdom, which shall never be destroyed: and the kingdom shall not be left to other people, but it shall break in pieces and consume all these kingdoms, and it shall stand for ever. Forasmuch as thou sawest that the stone was cut out of the mountain without hands, and that it brake in pieces the iron, the brass, the clay, the silver, and the gold; the great God hath made known to the king what shall come to pass hereafter: and the dream is certain, and the interpretation thereof sure* (Dan. 2:44, 45, emphasis mine).

Daniel's interpretation of Nebuchadnezzar's forgotten dream not only caused the king to spare Daniel's life and the lives of his friends, but it also lifted him to an important position in the government of Babylon. This man of God would now have influence throughout the world, and his prophecies would never be forgotten.

Daniel's Vision

The prophet Daniel interpreted Nebuchadnezzar's dream when he was a very young man. Nearly forty years later he was given a vision that confirmed and further explained his first preview of the future. In this vision Daniel saw the major world empires represented by four beasts (Dan. 7).

The first beast was like a lion with eagle's wings (7:4).

The second was like a bear that raised itself on one side, having three ribs in its mouth (7:5).

The third was like a leopard, having four wings and four heads (7:6).

The fourth was described as "dreadful and terrible, and strong exceedingly." It had ten horns and after a time another little horn grew and plucked up three of the other horns by the roots. The little horn had eyes like a man and a mouth speaking great things (7:7, 8).

What do these four beasts signify? Could they be interpreted in the light of nations now on the world scene? Is the lion with eagle's wings a reference to the British Empire and the United States, as some contend? Is Daniel's bear really Russia? Does the leopard symbolize the African nations, since that area is the leopard's natural home?

If not, why not?

Historically, students of Bible prophecy have seen Daniel's vision as a further development of the preview given in Nebuchadnezzar's dream.

The reason? The context of the Scripture portion demands it.

27

The lion then represents Nebuchadnezzar's Babylonian Empire.

The bear finds fulfillment in the Medo-Persian Empire that followed. The bear was raised on one side because the Persians were stronger than the Medes. The three ribs in the bear's mouth indicate three major conquests of that empire.

The leopard, having four wings and four heads, was a prophetic picture of the Grecian Empire. Led by Alexander the Great, the Greeks were swift and devastating in their conquest of the Medes and Persians. Alexander declared himself emperor of the world and great honors were paid him. But the young military genius died in his early thirties and his empire was divided between his four generals, fulfilling the prophecy that the leopard would have four heads.

The fourth beast, described as "dreadful and terrible, and strong exceedingly," represents the Roman Empire.

Daniel's interpretation of his vision of the four beasts gives little explanation of the significance of the beasts themselves or the empires they represent. That is not strange since they are but an enlargement of his interpretation of Nebuchadnezzar's dream. But the prophet is fascinated by the ten horns, which correspond to the ten toes on the great image, and especially by the little horn that rises later, portraying a powerful leader in the end time.

Note Daniel's warning about this coming evil person:

And the ten horns out of this kingdom are ten kings that shall arise: and another shall rise after them; and he shall be diverse from the first, and he shall subdue three kings. And he shall speak great words against the most High, and shall wear out the saints of the most High, and think to change times and laws: and they shall be given into his hand until a time and times and the dividing of time (Dan. 7:24, 25).

Who is this persecutor whose evil power seems unchecked

for three and one-half years (a time and times and the dividing of time)? Why does the world accept him? Why is he allowed to bring such destruction? We will learn more about the earth's most evil ruler through the study of another of Daniel's prophecies, this one concerning his own people, the Jews.

The Seventy Weeks

When Daniel entered the court of Nebuchadnezzar he was a young man. Shortly thereafter he interpreted the king's dream, giving an outline of the future and showing the rise and fall of the major Gentile empires from that time until the end.

In mid-life he received the strange vision of beasts and kingdoms that substantiated and enlarged the prophecy of his youth. He was greatly exercised about the evil ruler who is yet to appear and who will assume immense power while persecuting the people of God.

Near the end of his life he found himself studying Jeremiah's prophecy and recalling that the captivity of his people was to last seventy years. Since that period had nearly elapsed, he began to pray about the return to Jerusalem. Mourning over the desolation of his homeland, he prayed for its restoration, confessing his own sins and the sins of his people.

During his prayer Daniel was visited by the angel Gabriel, who gave him a timetable of coming events that would especially affect Israel, his own people. The angelic message given to Daniel is known as the vision of the seventy weeks. This mathematical revelation gave the Jews the exact time at which to expect the coming of their Messiah. It also prophesied His death and foretold the coming destruction of Jerusalem following His crucifixion, as well as the rise of the Antichrist and the establishment of Christ's coming kingdom on earth. Read this amazing prophecy:

Seventy weeks are determined upon thy people and upon thy

holy city, to finish the transgression, and to make an end of sins, and to make reconciliation for iniquity, and to bring in everlasting righteousness, and to seal up the vision of prophecy, and to anoint the most Holy. Know therefore and understand, that from the going forth of the commandment to restore and to build Jerusalem unto the Messiah the Prince shall be seven weeks, and threescore and two weeks: the street shall be built again, and the wall, even in troublous times. And after three- score and two weeks shall Messiah be cut off, but not for himself: and the people of the prince that shall come shall destroy the city and the sanctuary; and the end thereof shall be with a flood, and unto the end of the war desolations are determined. And he shall confirm the covenant with many for one week: and in the midst of the week he shall cause the sacrifice and the oblation to cease, and for the overspreading of abomina- tions he shall make it desolate, even until the consummation, and that determined shall be poured upon the desolate (Dan. 9:24-27).

Sir Edward Denny, a respected nineteenth-century student of prophecy, referred to the vision of the seventy weeks as the backbone of prophecy. It may well be just that.

The importance of the prophecy is stressed by Alva J. McClain in his book *Daniel's Prophecy of the Seventy Weeks,* in which he wrote:

"...only an omniscient God could have foretold over five hundred years in advance the very day on which the Messiah would ride into Jerusalem and present Himself as the "Prince" of Israel. Yet this is precisely what has been done in the prophecy of the Seventy Weeks." [2]

There are two important facts to remember while studying the prophecy.

First, this is a prophecy concerning Israel: "*Seventy weeks are determined upon thy people*" (Dan. 9:24).

Second, the word translated "weeks" literally means "sevens" and does not refer to a week of seven *days*. The angel announced to Daniel that seventy "sevens" were determined upon the people of Israel.

What were these "sevens"?

The context clearly shows them to be sets of seven *years*. Daniel had just been considering the *years* of the captivity of his people and had read Jeremiah's prophecy that said the captivity would last for seventy years. The seventy years of captivity were years of chastening for not allowing the land to have its Sabbaths for 490 years. The land was granted its Sabbaths during the absence of the Jews. The context is not only *years*, but another seventy weeks of years, or 490 *years*. There is no question about the length of time here intended—490 *years*.

But 490 years from when? And to accomplish what?

The vision is clear. The 490-year count would begin when the commandment went forth to restore and build Jerusalem. That is a date that has been preserved for us in the Bible.

When the time came for the Jews to return to their land, Nehemiah asked King Artaxerxes for permission to go to Jerusalem to rebuild the city. The king issued the decree to restore and build Jerusalem as Nehemiah requested. It is a thrilling story, especially since it begins by recording the date of Nehemiah's request and the forthcoming decree:

And it came to pass in the month Nisan, in the twentieth year of Artaxerxes the king, that wine was before him: and I took up wine, and gave it unto the king. Now I had not been beforetime sad in his presence. Wherefore the king said unto me, Why is thy countenance sad, seeing thou art not sick? this is nothing else but sorrow of heart. Then I was very sore afraid, And said unto the king, Let the king live for ever: why should not my

31

countenance be sad, when the city, the place of my fathers' sep-
ulchers, lieth waste, and the gates thereof are consumed with
fire? Then said the king unto me, For what dost thou make
request? So I prayed to the God of heaven. And I said unto the
king, If it please the king, and if thy servant have found favor
in thy sight, that thou wouldest send me unto Judah, unto the
city of my fathers' sepulchers, that I may build it. And the king
said unto me, (the queen also sitting by him,) For how long
shall thy journey be? and when wilt thou return? So it pleased
the king to send me; and I set him a time. Moreover I said
unto the king, If it please the king, let letters be given me to the
governors beyond the river, that they may convey me over till
I come into Judah; And a letter unto Asaph the keeper of the
king's forest, that he may give me timber to make beams for the
gates of the palace which appertained to the house, and for the
wall of the city, and for the house that I shall enter into. And
the king granted me, according to the good hand of my God
upon me (Nehemiah 2:1-8, emphasis mine).

Note that important date again—the twentieth year of King
Artaxerxes. Since the king had taken the throne in 465 B.C., his
twentieth year would have been 445 B.C. The month the decree
was issued was Nisan. Since the day is not given, Jewish custom
demands it to have been the first day of the month. Translating
the date given in the Bible to our calendar, the king's decree to
rebuild Jerusalem went forth on March 14, 445 B.C.

At first glance, then, it would appear that 490 years from
March 14, 445 B.C. should have brought the end of transgressions, reconciliation for iniquity, the beginning of everlasting
righteousness, the fulfilling of all prophecy, and the crowning of
the Messiah as King (Dan. 9:24).

But wait! There is a time break in the prophecy. After sixty-
nine weeks (483 years) the Messiah would come as the Prince
but He would be rejected and cut off.

That is exactly what happened.

Precisely 483 years after the issuing of the decree to build Jerusalem, the Messiah came riding into Jerusalem as had been prophesied:

Rejoice greatly, O daughter of Zion; shout, O daughter of Jerusalem: behold, thy King cometh unto thee: he is just, and having salvation; lowly, and riding upon an ass, and upon a colt the foal of an ass (Zech. 9:9).

Messiah the Prince was rejected by His people. He was cut off (crucified), but not for Himself; He died for others.

At the moment of Jesus' death the prophetic clock stopped ticking as far as this vision for Israel is concerned, for it deals with that time in history when God interacts specifically with that nation. Through the death of Christ, the wall between Jews and Gentiles was broken down. In this church age, Jews and Gentiles become one in Christ at the moment of new birth;

But now in Christ Jesus ye who sometimes were far off are made nigh by the blood of Christ. For he is our peace, who hath made both one, and hath broken down the middle wall of partition between us; Having abolished in his flesh the enmity, even the law of commandments contained in ordinances; for to make in himself of twain one new man, so making peace (Eph. 2:13-15).

The prophetic clock will remain silent, leaving one week of years unfulfilled, until the church makes its exit from the earth at the return of Christ—the Rapture. Israel will then again become the object of God's special dealing; the final seven years of Daniel's vision will be counted off in the world's most terrible time.

The final stages of Daniel's prophecies will all find fulfillment simultaneously.

Ten nations that once were part of the Roman Empire will

join together in an economic and political alliance.

The "little horn speaking great things" will emerge as a powerful political leader to whom three national heads of the new European federation will give full allegiance. Soon the other seven leaders will follow, making this evil man a dictator of immense power.

This newly acclaimed head of the revived Roman Empire will sign a seven-year peace treaty with Israel but will break it in the middle of the seventieth week—the middle of the final seven years:

> *And he shall confirm the covenant with many for one week: and in the midst of the week he shall cause the sacrifice and the oblation to cease, and for the overspreading of abominations he shall make it desolate, even until the consummation, and that determined shall be poured upon the desolate* (Dan. 9:27).

Those will be traumatic days for Israel. Just when peace seems to have come, it will be taken from her and she will be plunged into another bloody persecution.

What are the ingredients in the mixture of time and circumstances that will produce such a devastating explosion of persecution and misery for Israel at closing time?

And why has this particular nation suffered so much?

3
WEEP FOR YOUR CHILDREN

Daughters of Jerusalem, weep not for me, but weep for ...your children (Luke 23:28).

The Jews missed their Messiah. He walked among them and they did not recognize Him, even though their prophets had described His coming in great detail. His ancestry was to be in the family of David. His coming was to be announced by one who was known as a "voice crying in the wilderness." His birthplace was to be Bethlehem. He was to be born of a virgin. He was to be the eternal God incarnate. He was to minister to the poor and needy. He was to be presented to Israel as the Prince at the time prescribed in Daniel's vision of the seventy weeks. He was to be despised and rejected. He was to die for others by crucifixion. He was to be resurrected. Following His death, and in the lifetime of those who rejected and crucified Him, Jerusalem was to be destroyed and its citizens scattered and persecuted. Ultimately He would end war and establish a government of equity and justice, headquartered at Jerusalem. He would bring peace to Israel and to the world. Did Jesus Christ fulfill these ancient prophecies?

Roots

And there shall come forth a rod out of the stem of Jesse, and a Branch shall grow out of his roots (Isaiah 11:1).

Dr. Luke, who was chosen to give the most complete account

of the birth of Christ, records that Jesus was born of the family of David. The third chapter of his Gospel gives a complete genealogy of Mary, the mother of Jesus, tracing her ancestry through David (Luke 3:23-38).

The angel Gabriel was sent to announce the birth of Jesus. Luke says the heavenly messenger was sent to "*a virgin espoused to a man whose name was Joseph, of the house of David; and the virgin's name was Mary*" (Luke 1:27).

The ancestry of Jesus was known so well to His contemporaries that some who came to seek help and healing referred to Him as the "son of David." "*And when Jesus departed thence, two blind men followed him, crying, and saying, Thou son of David, have mercy on us*" (Matt. 9:27). After one of His miracles of healing, many were ready to accept Jesus as the Promised One. They made an unmistakable reference to Him as the "son of David" of whom the prophets had written, asking, "*Is not this the son of David?*" (Matt. 12:23). But the religious leaders rebuked them, saying He had performed the miracle in the power of Satan.

The Voice in the Wilderness

The voice of him that crieth in the wilderness, Prepare ye the way of the Lord, make straight in the desert a highway for our God (Isaiah 40:3).

Sometimes we forget there were two miraculous births connected with the Incarnation. Although John the Baptist was not born of a virgin, his birth was miraculous in that it was a fulfillment of prophecy and an answer to prayer. John was sent to prepare the way of the Lord.

John is called a "voice." And what a voice he was! Multitudes came to hear him. Even the king stood in his audience. He was an unusual man, fearless and faithful. His boldness cost him his head, but not until his work was done. We know him as the "forerunner of Christ."

It is important to notice that in Isaiah's prophecy of John the Baptist's mission, he is said to have come preparing the way of the LORD (40:3). Here all the letters in "Lord," have been capitalized, showing that John came to prepare the way of Jehovah, an inescapable declaration of the deity of Christ.

Bethlehem

But thou, Bethlehem Ephratah, though thou be little among the thousands of Judah, yet out of thee shall he come forth unto me that is to be ruler in Israel; whose goings forth have been from of old, from everlasting (Micah 5:2).

Micah the prophet had revealed that the Messiah would be born in Bethlehem. Joseph and Mary lived in Nazareth. How would this problem be solved?

The Roman government enacted a law that called for every man to return to the city of his family to pay his taxes, providing a census as well as taxation. It was therefore necessary for Joseph and Mary to leave Nazareth and go to Bethlehem, because he was of the family of David. The mighty Roman Empire unwittingly became a partner in fulfilling the prophecy concerning both the time and place of the birth of the Messiah.

And Christ was born in Bethlehem.

The Virgin Birth—God Incarnate

Therefore the Lord himself shall give you a sign; Behold, a virgin shall conceive, and bear a son, and shall call his name Immanuel (Isaiah 7:14).

For centuries the Jews had awaited the coming of the Messiah. Longing to be free from foreign domination, they especially anticipated the fulfillment of messianic promises that

37

concerned lasting peace and the restoration of David's kingdom. When prophetic voices ceased for four hundred years, some doubted.

Suddenly the silence was broken. Angels went on missions of earthshaking importance. John the Baptist was to come (Luke 1:5-25). Christ would be born (Luke 1:26-38).

The angel Gabriel brought the announcement of the coming birth of Jesus to Mary, who was engaged to Joseph. She would conceive as a result of a miracle of the Holy Spirit and give birth to the "*Son of the Highest*," who would sit upon "*the throne of His father David*" (Luke 1:32).

When it became evident that Mary was with child, Joseph was beside himself. The emotional trauma might have destroyed him had not an angel been sent to give him guidance. Explaining the miracle that was happening in Mary, the heavenly agent advised Joseph to proceed with the planned marriage, assuring him that the child conceived in her was of the Holy Spirit.

Here human understanding falters. Even Mary asked, "*How shall this be, seeing I know not a man?*" (Luke 1:34). Nevertheless, students of the Old Testament know this miracle had been prophesied. Its fulfillment should have been another reason for accepting the Messiah when He came.

Bible students who doubt the virgin birth of Christ are themselves a contradiction. They wrestle with the sign, yet often claim to accept the Savior. There is no question but that the virgin birth required God's intervention. The name "Immanuel," given by Isaiah, shows that the child would be God robed in flesh. Immanuel means "God with us."

By pinpointing Bethlehem as the Messiah's birthplace, Micah makes certain that his readers will understand just who is being born in David's city. He is identified as the One whose "*goings forth have been from of old, from everlasting*" (Micah 5:2).

The Messiah was born of a virgin in Bethlehem, as had been promised by the prophets of Israel. And the world was confronted with the Incarnation of the eternal God.

Ministering to the Poor and Needy

The Spirit of the Lord God is upon me; because the LORD hath anointed me to preach good tidings unto the meek; he hath sent me to bind up the brokenhearted, to proclaim liberty to the captives, and the opening of the prison to them that are bound; To proclaim the acceptable year of the LORD, and the day of vengeance of our God; to comfort all that mourn (Isaiah 61:1,2).

In the early part of His ministry, Jesus entered the synagogue in Nazareth on the Sabbath day and read this prophecy. Upon finishing, He closed the book, gave it to the minister, and sat down. As all eyes turned to Him, He said: *"This day is this scripture fulfilled in your ears"* (Luke 4:21).

The years that followed demonstrated the truth of His statement. The poor and needy came to Him and He received them. Lepers were cleansed. The blind were given sight. Lame men walked. Grieving people had loved ones restored to life, Even little children were not overlooked; He laid His hands on them and prayed for them.

The Messiah was a man of compassion, seeing people as sheep without a shepherd and longing to gather them to Himself as a hen gathers her chicks when sheltering them from danger. The rich and self-righteous were often bitter about His holy life and resented His authority in preaching, but the common people heard Him gladly.

Rejection

He is despised and rejected of men... (Isaiah 53:3).

Desire sometimes colors judgment. Prophecies concerning the Messiah should have prepared the people both for His suffering and for His earthly kingdom of peace and justice. But the majority of Jews thought only of the glories of the messianic reign and the benefits it would bring to Israel.

Ignoring prophecies concerning the Messiah's meekness and mercy and concentrating only on His might and power, Jewish leaders formed a picture of the Promised One that did not fit the gentle Jesus who went about ministering to the sick and taking time for little children. Their dreams of liberation and political power caused them to be blind to the total message of their prophets about the Messiah.

When He came, they despised Him.

They taunted Him with questions, hoping to embarrass Him publicly. They incited the people to riot and persuaded them to attempt His murder by stoning. They slandered Him with subtle comments about His virgin birth. They mocked His claims to deity and demanded He show some sign of His authority. They attributed His miracles to the devil. Finally, they collaborated with one of His disciples to betray him for thirty pieces of silver, another fulfillment of prophecy: *"And I said unto them, If ye think good, give me my price; and if not, forbear. So they weighed for my price thirty pieces of silver"* (Zech. 11:12).

Crucifixion

But he was wounded for our transgressions, he was bruised for our iniquities: the chastisement of our peace was upon him; and with his stripes we are healed (Isaiah 53:5).

The suffering and death of Christ should not have come as a surprise to those who awaited the coming of the Messiah. Isaiah referred to Him as a lamb brought to the slaughter. He also described the suffering and shame the Messiah would be subjected to just before His death on the cross: *"I gave my back to the smiters and my cheeks to them that plucked off the hair: I hid not my face from shame and spitting"* (Isaiah 50:6).

This same prophet wrote of the silence of the Savior before His persecutors and revealed that His grave would be with the wicked and the rich. Jesus was crucified between two thieves and buried in the tomb of the wealthy Joseph of Arimathea. Isaiah described the death of Christ and explained its significance seven hundred years before it took place.

Daniel foresaw the Messiah's death and prophesied that He would be *"cut off, but not for himself" (Dan. 9:26).*

Zechariah wrote of the piercing of Jesus' body and said He would receive wounds in His hands: *"...and they shall look upon me whom they have pierced..."* (Zech. 12:10). *"And one shall say unto him, What are these wounds in thine hands? Then he shall answer, Those with which I was wounded in the house of my friends"* (Zech. 13:6).

Perhaps the most remarkable prophecy having to do with the Messiah's death is David's description of crucifixion given in Psalm 22. Here the coming death of Christ on a cross is depicted about eight hundred years before that method of execution was used by the Romans. The Jews knew nothing of crucifixion at that time; capital punishment was carried out by stoning.

Beginning with the very words the Messiah would cry from the cross ("My God, my God, why hast thou forsaken me?"), this Psalm accurately expresses the agonies of that awful death. In his book, *Christ in the Psalms,* the late Dr. William Pettingill calls Psalm 22 the "Psalm of Sobs," saying it is a picture of our Lord's crucifixion written a thousand years before the event.

The footnote given in the *New Scofield Reference Bible* on Psalm 22 is excellent:

"Psalm 22 is a graphic picture of death by crucifixion. The bones (of the hands, arms, shoulders, and pelvis) out of joint

(v. 14); the profuse perspiration caused by intense suffering (v. 14); the action of the heart affected (v. 14); strength exhausted, and extreme thirst (v. 15); the hands and feet pierced (see v. 16); partial nudity with the hurt to modesty (v. 17), are all associated with that mode of death. The accompanying circumstances are precisely those fulfilled in the crucifixion of Christ..." [1]

Resurrection

For thou wilt not leave my soul in hell; neither wilt thou suffer thine Holy One to see corruption (Ps. 16:10).

The apostles Peter and Paul both identify the above verse as a prophecy of the resurrection of Christ (Acts 2:27;13:35).

Jesus prophesied His resurrection and called it the sign of His deity. When questioned about His power to perform miracles and to minister with authority, He replied: *"Destroy this temple, and in three days I will raise it up"* (John 2:19).

The Savior openly announced His coming resurrection to His disciples (Matt. 16:21), but after His death the disciples seemed to forget that promise.

His enemies had better memories. They petitioned Pilate for a guard at the tomb. Attempts to prevent the resurrection were futile, however, and the security measures taken by unbelievers only added to the evidence that proved He arose. The tomb was empty in spite of the Roman guard placed there. And the resurrection of Jesus has become one of the best-attested facts of history.

The Destruction of Jerusalem

The rejection of the Messiah by the Jews brought Him untold suffering. But those who rejected and crucified Him also suffered. Foreseeing the sorrows that would come to those who chose unbelief, He wept and warned. Desperate days were ahead for His persecutors and He mourned over their coming calamities.

On the day of His triumphal entry into Jerusalem, on the day prophesied by Daniel in his vision of the seventy weeks, Jesus said through tears:

If thou hadst known, even thou, at least in this thy day, the things which belong unto thy peace! but now they are hid from thine eyes. For the days shall come upon thee, that thine enemies shall cast a trench before thee, and compass thee round, and keep thee in on every side, And shall lay thee even with the ground, and thy children within thee; and they shall not leave in thee one stone upon another; because thou knewest not the time of thy visitation (Luke 19:42-44).

As the time of His betrayal and crucifixion drew near, His warnings of coming destruction grew more intense:

And when ye shall see Jerusalem compassed with armies, then know that the desolation thereof is nigh. Then let them which are in Judea flee to the mountains; and let them which are in the midst of it depart out; and let not them that are in the countries enter thereinto. For these be the days of vengeance, that all things which are written may be fulfilled. But woe to them that are with child, and to them that give suck, in those days! for there shall be great distress in the land, and wrath upon this people. And they shall fall by the edge of the sword, and shall be led away captive into all nations: and Jerusalem shall be trodden down of the Gentiles, until the times of the Gentiles be fulfilled (Luke 21:20-24).

Israel had experienced chastisement for unbelief in the past. Because of their lack of faith and unwillingness to enter the land to which Moses had led them, they had wandered in the wilderness for forty years, permitting an entire generation to die. As a result

43

of their disobedience and neglect of the commandments, they were taken captive by the Assyrians and the Babylonians. Now in the rejection of their Messiah they would secure their longest and most severe judgment. Jerusalem would be destroyed, the temple leveled, and the people scattered, killed, and made slaves. And the beginning of these sorrows would take place in the lifetime of those who shared in Jesus' crucifixion.

Did it happen?

History is witness to the total fulfillment of this frightening prophecy.

In A.D. 66 the Jews revolted against Roman rule because of heavy taxation. They massacred the Roman garrison at Jerusalem, bringing the wrath of Rome upon them. The governor of Syria marched with his army against Jerusalem to bring the Jews into line but did not have enough men to put down the uprising and so did not attack. Instead, the city was put under siege.

The burning of Rome and the death of Nero prevented settling the problem for some time. The awful siege brought famine and chaos, but the Jews held out.

Finally, in A.D. 70, a Roman general named Vespasian was sent to take command of the army and put down the rebellion. However, at the death of Nero he was called back to Rome to be made the emperor and his son Titus was given charge of the army and assigned the task of taking Jerusalem.

When Titus and his army entered the city they were ruthless. Roman soldiers cut down all the trees in the area that were suitable for crucifixions and carried out hundreds of executions. Josephus the historian says that 1,100,000 Jews were slain and thousands of others taken into captivity. Many were sold as slaves and some were sent to be used as gladiators to fight wild beasts for the entertainment of those in Rome.

Titus had hoped to save the temple, but the Jews chose that location as their last point of resistance, perhaps hoping for the Messiah to come and deliver them in the final hour of struggle.

During the battle, a Roman soldier set fire to the magnificent structure, bringing about its total destruction. Even the stones of the temple were pried apart in an effort to salvage precious metals that had melted between them.

Many years before this tragic hour, the Messiah of Israel had turned to speak to a group of weeping women who were following Him down the road to Calvary where He would be crucified. *"Daughters of Jerusalem,"* He said, *"weep not for me, but weep for yourselves, and for your children."*

Now it was A.D. 70 and the weeping had begun.

A trail of tears would follow the Jewish people through the centuries. We will walk with them through their incredible sufferings, as they struggle on toward a return to their homeland, the acceptance of their rejected Messiah, and ultimate peace.

4
WOULD GOD
IT WERE MORNING!

And thy life shall hang in doubt before thee; and thou shalt fear day and night, and shalt have none assurance of thy life: In the morning thou shalt say, Would God it were even! and at even thou shalt say, Would God it were morning!...(Deut. 28:66,67).

Dispersion

Dispersion was not new to the Jews. Captivity had been God's method of correcting them in the past.

The Assyrians had taken the Northern Kingdom captive in about 722 B.C.. Some years later, in 586 B.C., Nebuchadnezzar and the Babylonians conquered Jerusalem and took the remainder of the people to Babylon. The Babylonian Empire covered essentially the same area as had the Assyrian Empire. After seventy years of captivity, a remnant of the Jews returned to their land to rebuild the temple and the city of Jerusalem.

Before his death, Moses had warned his people that dispersion, captivity, and persecution would come to them if they did not obey the laws of God. His prophecy was a disturbing one, dealing with intense sorrow and suffering for the Jews. If disobedient, they were to expect extreme poverty, the loss of property, and conquest by a nation of awesome military might. They would be looked down upon and de-spised by other nations. Finally, experiencing a worldwide dispersion, they would be uneasy, unhappy, and afraid:

And among these nations shall thou find no ease, neither shall the sole of thy foot have rest: but the LORD shall give thee there a trembling heart, and failing of eyes, and sorrow of mind: And thy life shall hang in doubt before thee; and thou shalt fear day and night, and shalt have none assurance of thy life (Deut. 28:65,66).

Following the rejection of their Messiah and the dispersion after the destruction of Jerusalem, the Jews entered upon their longest period of suffering and persecution. Sixty years after the leveling of Jerusalem there was an attempt by a sizable number of Jews to return to their land, but this abortive move was doomed to failure and more than one-half million were massacred.

Dispersion was definite—irreversible at that time.

The Hunted

During the period between the resurrection of Christ and the destruction of Jerusalem, the Jews imprisoned and executed many Christians. But now they were the hunted. Imprisonment, slavery, and death became their lot. At one time, so many of them were sold into slavery that the slave markets were glutted with Jews and there were not enough buyers to purchase them.

Even this unhappy situation had been prophesied by Moses: *"And the Lord shall bring thee into Egypt again with ships, by the way whereof I spake unto thee, Thou shalt see it no more again: and there ye shall be sold unto your enemies for bondmen and bond-women, and no man shall buy you"* (Deut. 28:68).

We who live within memory of the Nazi nightmare, when six million Jews died in Europe, might conclude that Hitler's hatred of this people was a phenomenon of the twentieth century. Not so, for Jewish blood had been spilled across Europe and in other parts of the world for centuries. In taking the long look at history, one sees that the Jews had been steadily marching toward Hitler's ovens ever since the fall of their beloved city in A.D. 70.

Pauses in Persecution

There were, however, periods of respite.

Although they were scattered, afflicted, and unhappy in most parts of the world, the Jews found a temporary haven in Spain. Here Jews worked, studied, and engaged in commerce alongside their neighbors. During this time, a considerable amount of Jewish literature was produced in both Hebrew and Arabic. Moses Maimonides (1135-1204), considered by many to be the greatest of all medieval Jewish writers, did his work then. This era of relative calm is known as 'The Golden Age Of Spanish Jewry."

But it did not last.

Waves of fanatical Muslim Berbers from North Africa began to disturb the Jewish life style. Following that, invaders from the north conquered all of Spain and oppression once again became a way of life for the Jews. Although we remember 1492 as the year of the discovery of America by Columbus, it was also the time in history at which the Jews in Spain experienced untold suffering in a reign of Spanish terror. At the decree of Ferdinand and Isabella, 800,000 Jews were packed into boats and set adrift to die. Most did. Before the year was over, the remaining Jews were expelled from Spain. The Golden Age of Spanish Jewry had ended.

Jews fleeing from persecution in a number of European nations found the Rhine Valley a friendly place for a time, and they settled there by the thousands. It seemed that the Jews had found another homeland, a European land of promise.

But even there misery overtook them. Crusaders passing through the Rhineland on their way to the Middle East thought it their obligation to God to destroy as many Jews as possible. Attacking without mercy, their battle cry was "Deus Vult," meaning "God wills it." The Crusaders slaughtered Jews throughout Europe and upon arriving in the Middle East they continued their carnage, even burning Jews alive in their synagogues.

It seems impossible that such acts could have been committed in the name of Christianity. But that dark hour is an unforgettable example of the tragedies that can occur when professing Christians fanatically follow leaders who do not know the teachings of the Bible.

The Universal Scapegoat

Everywhere the Jews were blamed for the ills of their day.

Some still foolishly follow that practice. In the twentieth century, Jews are accused of controlling all money, causing all depressions, influencing spiraling inflation, and plotting the conquest of the world. Some generally assume that Jews own everything.

There is nothing new under the sun; Jew accusers today are simply following the lead of anti-Semitics before them. People who do not wish to accept responsibility for the wrongs in society must have a scapegoat, and the Jews have been a universal scapegoat. They take the blame of ignorant people for problems ranging from plagues to politics.

Incredibly, even the awful plague of the Black Death that swept Europe was blamed on the Jews. They were accused of having poisoned wells with a powder made of spiders, frog legs, Christian entrails, and consecrated hosts (Communion bread). The public wrath that resulted from that fantastic tale brought about the slaughter of thousands of Jews and the complete extermination of two hundred Jewish communities. This fierce hatred of Jews and the willingness to believe such outlandish accusations against them can only be explained as a fulfillment of Moses' prophecy: "*And thou shalt become an astonishment, a proverb, and a byword, among all nations whither the LORD shall lead thee*" (Deut. 28:37).

Poland became the next inviting oasis in the desert of Jewish persecution and dispersion. After being attacked and slaughtered in their beloved Rhine Valley by the Crusaders, many Jews fled to Poland. Encouraged there by kings Boleslav the Pious and Casimer the Great, they established a community that continued into the twentieth century, ending in the "holocaust" of World War II.

The Jews who settled in Poland seemed to have found a stable sanctuary. There they were able to practice their Hebrew customs and even were allowed to use their own languages — Hebrew for religious practices and Yiddish for secular life. They were granted partial political autonomy under the Polish crown and were governed by their own supreme council, known as the Council of the Four Lands. Legal problems between Jews were settled by their own rabbinical courts instead of by Polish law.

Bible prophecies of suffering and persecution appeared to have overlooked the nearly ideal conditions the Jews were experiencing in Poland. They began to relax and feel safe. The persecutions of the past were far removed from them. Their lives were no longer in jeopardy. They were prospering financially.

But the prophet's words were not to be denied. In the eighteenth century, much of eastern Poland became part of the Russian Empire and the quality of life for Jews there began to decline. Their autonomy was eroded. Once again came unwanted domination. They were hounded and persecuted by czarist authorities and were confined to areas consisting mainly of small towns along the Russian and Polish borders.

In the latter part of the nineteenth century, under Czar Alexander III, the persecution became almost unbearable. It was then that a new word entered the vocabulary of Jews and Russians: "pogrom." This word was adopted by the czars as a name for organized massacres of Jews carried out by soldiers who burned and murdered their way through Jewish settlements in western Russia. Moses' warning that they would never find a place of ease must have come to mind as this battered people prepared for another exodus, this time from Russia.

Fleeing westward, many Jews arrived in the United Kingdom and the United States of America. Seventy-five percent of the Jews in the United Kingdom and the United States are of Russian descent.

Social and economic sanctions were brought against the Jews in nearly every nation. Many countries barred Jews from owning land. They were not allowed to join craft guilds. At one time they were expelled from both England and France and all of their property was confiscated. The church forbade Jews to employ Christians and Christians to live among Jews.

The Fourth Lateran Council of 1215 demanded that all Jews wear a distinguishing badge. In England, Jews wore a replica of the tablets on which the Ten Commandments were given. France and Germany demanded a yellow "0" not unlike the yellow stars used by the Nazis in marking the Jews for gas chambers.

In Germany Jews were forbidden to ride in carriages and were forced to pay a toll whenever they entered a city. In Venice, Jews were required to live in a particular area; the word used to designate their forced boundaries is the one from which we get the word "ghetto."

In Russia, Jews were drafted for military service at the age of twelve and had to serve for twenty-five years. They were also forced to pay special taxes on kosher meat and Sabbath candles. Jewish women living in large city university centers were required to wear the mark of a prostitute. And even these miseries had been foretold long ago:

> *Thou shalt beget sons and daughters, but thou shalt not enjoy them; for they shall go into captivity. . . . The stranger that is within thee shall get up above thee very high; and thou shalt come down very low. He shall lend to thee, and thou shalt not lend to him: he shall be the head, and thou shalt be the tail* (Deut. 28:41,43,44).

51

The Human Side of History

The magnitude of Jewish sufferings is difficult to take in completely. One may read of sanctions, slaughters, persecutions, and prejudices, but these are likely to simply move through the mind as historic facts without telling the whole story. The real account of the miseries of the Jews is one of feelings, frustrations, and fears. That is the human side of history.

Who can measure the hurt in being stigmatized, ridiculed, set apart, and hated? Imagine the horror of being separated from loved ones and sold as a slave. Think of living under the constant threat of death, as did the Jews during the Cossack rebellion when 100,000 of them died through torture and violence in less than a decade. Feel the grief of Jewish families when 1,500 of their relatives were executed in York, England, in one day under the decree of King John. (How ironic that New York has become the city with the world's largest Jewish population.)

Even in America, Jews have been the subject of jokes and ridicule. Here too the children of Israel have endured cutting remarks and de facto segregation. Now that Arab oil is necessary for Americans to continue their love affair with affluence and travel, one wonders how long this nation will officially stand on the side of the Jews. Perhaps the lust for black gold will end the "Golden Age of American Jewry." Can it be that the United States is about to become another Spain, or Rhine Valley, or Poland? Jewish favor has always been fragile, and oil may grease the slide in America. If so, the "Land of the Free" is about to enter its darkest hour.

Since the rejection and crucifixion of their Messiah, the story of the Jews has been one of misery. For many, life itself has been a burden, a thing to wish away. As Moses put it, "*In the morning thou shalt say, Would God it were even! and at even thou shalt say, Would God it were morning! .. .*" (Deut. 28:67).

Those who have wronged the Jews have fared no better than

those they have persecuted. History's graveyards are filled with kings and generals who thought they could mistreat the Jews and get away with it. Actually, Jew-hating is a depraved luxury no nation can afford. In his book. *The World's Collision,* Dr. Charles E. Pont put it well:

> *Anti-Semites are not only the enemies of the Jews, they are their own enemies and the enemies of mankind. . . . All from Pharaoh to Hitler have been horribly judged for having fashioned a sword against these people. Czarist Russia came to an inglorious end as did Hitlerism and Fascism. Many of these loud-mouthed anti-Semites either committed suicide or were slain. . . . But what about the children of Israel? Like Old Man River they seem to roll along in spite of it all."* [1]

Long ago Abraham, the father of the Jewish race, was given an unusual promise by his Lord. This guarantee of blessing provided judgment upon all who would bring evil upon his descendents:

> *And I will make of thee a great nation, and I will bless thee, and make thy name great; and thou shalt be a blessing: And I will bless them that bless thee, and curse him that curseth thee: and in thee shall all families of the earth be blessed* (Gen. 12:2,3).

Frederick the Great said, "No nation ever persecuted the Jew and prospered." His correct observation is proof of God's faithfulness in keeping His promise to Abraham. Nebuchadnezzar, Herod, Titus, the Czars, Hitler, and scores of others are witnesses to this truth. The Jews are here to stay.

But there is another dimension of this story. The dispersion of the Jews will not last forever. Through the long and difficult years of their sufferings, the words of their prophets have continued to remind this scattered people that they would ultimately return to their land and there prosper under the leadership of their Messiah. To some, the idea seemed farfetched. But to others, this hope brought light in the darkest hours.

"Next year at Jerusalem" was heard year after year at Passover. Sometimes it had a hollow sound. Often those who spoke the words did not really believe them. Nevertheless, the promise of the prophets was passed on from one generation to another.

Finally a few dared do more than dream. An infant movement began that in less than a century would transport hundreds of thousands of Jews back to the land of then-fathers. After decades of struggle and war, a nation would be born, and it would be the most significant event of this century.

Who finally had the courage and vision to attempt the resurrection of the Jews, long buried in the nations to which they had wandered?

What events made the undertaking possible?

Which prophet gives the most moving description of the fulfillment of this stage-setting, end-time event?

Answering these questions will enrich our understanding of the sacred scene that is unfolding in these final hours of world history.

5
THE KNEE BONE
CONNECTED TO...

Queen Victoria asked her Jewish prime minister, Benjamin Disraeli, "Can you give me one verse in the Bible that will prove its truth?"

He replied, "Your Majesty, I will give you one word—Jew! If there was nothing else to prove the truth of the Bible, the history of the Jews is sufficient."

The survival of the Jews is a miracle. Scattered among the nations, despised by kings and generals who tried to destroy them, they have endured as a people. Why?

A Date with Destiny

The reason for the preservation of the Jewish race is found in the Bible. While their trials were foretold by the ancient prophets, so was their ultimate triumph. The same Book that announced their coming dispersion guaranteed their return to the land God had promised them: "*Hear the word of the LORD, O ye nations, and declare it in the isles afar off, and say, He that scattered Israel will gather him, and keep him, as a shepherd doth his flock*" (Jeremiah 31:10).

So the future of the Jews has always been sure. Efforts to destroy them as a race have been futile because they are destined to play an important role in end-time events. Actually, the Jews have been and still remain the most secure race on earth. The Hamans and Hitlers of history have come and gone, but the Jews remain. That is consistent with the message of the Bible: "*Though I make a full end of all nations whither I have scattered thee, yet will I not make a full end of thee: but I will correct thee in measure, and will not leave thee altogether unpunished*" (Jeremiah 30:11).

This tiny scattered people, moving through the nations of the world, has had such a definite date with destiny that no power on earth could destroy them.

Further, the future of Israel was pronounced by Jeremiah to be as certain as the laws of the universe:

> "*Thus saith the LORD, which giveth the sun for a light by day, and the ordinances of the moon and of the stars for a light by night, which divideth the sea when the waves thereof roar; The LORD of hosts is his name: If those ordinances depart from before me, saith the Lord, then the seed of Israel also shall cease from being a nation before me for ever. Thus saith the Lord; If heaven above can be measured, and the foundations of the earth searched out beneath, I will also cast off all the seed of Israel for all that they have done, saith the Lord*" (Jeremiah 31:35-37).

The ability of the Jews to remain a people apart while scattered throughout the world is another evidence of the divine plan. Minister and author Walter Brown Knight once wrote, "Through the centuries, the Jew has maintained his racial identity. Like Jonah in the belly of the great fish—undigested, unassimilated—the Jew has remained unassimilated, unamalgamated, undigested though he has wandered among all nations."

The Jews have been on a journey to Jerusalem for nearly two thousand years. Although at times some have lost sight of that destination in spite of their "Next year at Jerusalem" at Passover, the story of their sojourn through many lands and their ultimate return to the land of their fathers has been told again and again by the prophets.

Visit to a Cemetery

Perhaps the most vivid of all descriptions of the scattering and return of Israel is given by the prophet Ezekiel in his vision of the valley of dry bones. An acquaintance with this vision is essential to the student of prophecy who longs for an understanding of the events taking place in the Middle East in our day:

"The hand of the LORD was upon me, and carried me out in the spirit of the LORD, and set me down in the midst of the valley which was full of bones, And caused me to pass by them round about: and, behold, there were very many in the open valley; and, lo, they were very dry. And he said unto me, Son of man, can these bones live? And I answered, O Lord God, thou knowest. Again he said unto me, Prophesy upon these bones, and say unto them, O ye dry bones, hear the word of the Lord. Thus saith the Lord GOD unto these bones; Behold, I will cause breath to enter into you, and ye shall live: And I will lay sinews upon you, and will bring up flesh upon you, and cover you with skin, and put breath in you, and ye shall live; and ye shall know that I am the Lord. So I prophesied as I was commanded: and as I prophesied, there was a noise, and behold a shaking, and the bones came together, bone to his bone. And when I beheld, lo, the sinews and the flesh came up upon them, and the skin covered them above: but there was no breath in them. Then said he unto me, Prophesy unto the wind, prophesy, son of man, and say to the wind, Thus saith the Lord God; Come from the four winds, O breath, and breathe upon these slain, that they may live. So I prophesied as he commanded me, and the breath came into them, and they lived, and stood up upon their feet, an exceeding great army" (Ezekiel 37:1-10).

What an experience! The prophet was taken to a cemetery, a great valley full of bones. Exposed to the wind and sun, the bones had become dry and bleached. Ezekiel looked upon a valley full of skeletons, certainly not a happy sight, And while looking, he was asked: "Can these bones live?" In faith, he replied, "O Lord GOD, thou knowest."

Ezekiel was then given the responsibility of prophesying about these dry bones. He actually spoke to them and informed them that they would receive flesh, breath, and life. While he was speaking, there was a great noise and a shaking as the bones came together, attaching properly bone to bone. Finally, the skeletons, covered with flesh and given life, stood to their feet and became a great army. Further explaining the frightening experience, the prophet said:

> *"Then he said unto me, Son of man, these bones are the whole house of Israel: behold they say, Our bones are dried, and our hope is lost: we are cut off for our parts. Therefore prophesy and say unto them, Thus saith the Lord God; Behold, O my people, I will open your graves, and cause you to come up out of your graves, and bring you into the land of Israel. And ye shall know that I am the LORD, when I have opened your graves, O my people, and brought you up out of your graves, And shall put my spirit in you, and ye shall live, and I shall place you in your own land: then shall ye know that I the Lord have spoken it, and performed it, saith the Lord"* (Ezekiel 37:11-14).

Ezekiel's strange vision can be interpreted in this way: The bones represent Israel. Their disconnectedness and dryness indicate the people of Israel's scattering and lack of hope. The graves are the nations in which they dwell. The imparting of sinew, flesh, and breath is a miracle timed for the last days.

The Jews are to come out of their graves, i.e., the nations to which they have been scattered. They will return in unbelief and without spiritual life, but finally after being settled in their land, there will come a time of conversion—new birth:

"And ye shall know that I am the Lord, when I have opened your graves, O my people, and brought you up out of your graves, And shall put my spirit in you, and ye shall live, and I shall place you in your own land: then shall ye know that I the Lord have spoken it, and performed it, saith the Lord" (Ezekiel 37:13,14).

Understanding Ezekiel's vision is not difficult. But is it finding fulfillment in our day? Is there a point in time at which it can be reasonably said that the bones of Ezekiel's vision began coming together?

There is.

Following the ascension of Alexander III as Czar of Russia, thousands of Jews fled west in hope of finding freedom from persecution. Others turned their minds to nationalism. The ancient hope of a return to their homeland began to surface. To many, the thought seemed farfetched because Palestine was under Turkish control. Nevertheless, the desire of the Jews for a sanctuary moved them to establish two organizations, the purpose of both being the setting up of a Jewish homeland in the land of Palestine. Both groups were formed in 1882.

Birth of Zionism

The first of these organizations was called "Hoveve Zion," or "Lovers of Zion." This was a worldwide movement to promote interest in Jewish settlement in Palestine.

The second organization was a small group named "Bilu," composed of people who actually went to Palestine and began to work the land in spite of the objections of the Turks. The circumstances were very difficult and the settlements that were started were not economically successful. They were taken under the protection and assistance of Baron Edmund DeRothschild. In this way they survived.

The move among the Jews to return to their land, the stirring of the dry bones, was a small affair for more than a dozen years. In 1895, however, a dramatic event set one man's heart afire for the cause of Zionism. His name was Theodor Herzl.

Herzl, a Jewish Austrian newspaperman, had come to Paris to cover the public humiliation of Alfred Dreyfus, a French soldier convicted of collaboration with Germany. Dreyfus, a Jew, seemed the perfect example of one who had assimilated into the European culture and society, overcoming race and religion barriers. Having attended a famous military academy in France, he had received the rank of captain. Now he was accused of giving French military information to the German military attaché at Paris. Despite scanty evidence, a secret court-martial condemned Dreyfus to public humiliation and life imprisonment on Devil's Island. The case has gone down in history as a miscarriage of French justice.

The public humiliation of Dreyfus took place in January of 1895. Theodor Herzl stood with the crowd and heard them begin to cry, "Kill the traitor, kill the Jew." As the Jewish writer listened to the screams of the mob, a shock wave rolled through his entire being. Herzl heard that same crowd in effect crying for his blood, since he was also a Jew.

Walking away from the spectacle, Theodor Herzl was a broken man. Like Dreyfus, he had lived in comfort and had almost forgotten the persecutions of his people and the barriers that had existed between Jews and Gentiles through the centuries. Now he understood that those barriers still remained, that hatred for Jews was still real, and that all Jews were in jeopardy wherever they found themselves in the world. This awful awakening sent Herzl into seclusion to write a book that would shake the world and play an important role in establishing the State of Israel.

Herzl's book was a one-hundred-page work entitled: *Der Judenstaat—The Jewish State.* The book began: "The Jews who will it shall have a state of their own."

In 1897, two years after the publication of his book, Theodor Herzl called the first World Zionist Congress to session in Basle, Switzerland. The meeting was held in a gambling casino. The name of those determined to bring about the return to their land would now be "Zionists," so named for Mount Zion in Palestine. Herzl was elected the international executive. A Jewish fund was established as well as a land bank to make it possible to purchase land in Palestine. A flag was chosen. The colors were white and blue for the colors of the tallith prayer shawl, and "Hatikvah" (The Hope) was designated as a national anthem.

At the conclusion of that first Zionist Congress, Herzl wrote in his diary, "I have founded the Jewish state. If I were to say so today, people would laugh at me, but in five years' time, certainly in fifty years, it will be seen that I was right." (On November 29, 1947, almost fifty years after Herzl wrote the words, the General Assembly of the United Nations by a majority vote made the birth of the State of Israel legally possible. In May of 1948, the nation was born.)

The new leader of Zionism exhausted himself in the cause to which he was committed. During the next eight years he met with many of the world's statesmen. This leader of a homeless people had a vision of a modern-day exodus. He dreamed not of straggling groups finding their way back to the Jewish homeland, but rather of great companies of Jews settling in their land and prospering there.

Herzl spent much of his early effort seeking sponsoring nations among the European powers. His first thought was of Germany and he wooed Wilhelm II. Finding no help there, he turned to England. In 1903, one year before Herzl's death, the British offered the Jews the country of Uganda as a place to settle. Although the Jews rejected this African area, England's offer gave official recognition to the Jewish right of a homeland. Herzl counted that a great victory.

Shortly after the turn of the century, increased persecution in Russia sent many immigrants to Palestine. Herzl's work was bearing fruit. Among these Jewish settlers was a young man named David Green from Plonsk, a Polish town northwest of Warsaw. His father, an attorney, had been an avid Zionist and young Green had listened enthusiastically as his father discussed the merits of Zionism with his friends.

David Green was not content to simply debate the issues. He longed to live in Israel and had come there to contribute to the establishment of that nation. In their book, *O Jerusalem,* Larry Collins and Dominique Lapierre write that young Green found Jerusalem like a modern tower of Babel, with Jews speaking forty different languages and half of them unable to communicate with the other half.

Changing his name to David Ben-Gurion, this young immigrant became the editor of a Zionist trade union paper committed to the revival of the Hebrew language. After Herzl's death, he would become an important force in the establishment and development of the nation he loved.

The foundation of the nation had been laid. The dry bones were coming together. Ezekiel's vision was on its way to fulfillment; the most significant sign of the end times and the return of the Messiah would, in the next half century, become a reality.

But there were troubled times ahead.

War would come to Europe and to the world. Jews would find themselves in the middle of a global war, having friends on both sides of the conflict. The war itself would threaten to extinguish Zionism. For a time it would seem as if the bones of the vision would retreat to the dust and be as dry as the arid soil of the land the Jews were seeking to reclaim.

How did this struggling people manage to overcome the perils of World War I?

What part would World War I play in the development of the State of Israel and in setting the stage for the final drama of the ages?

What events in World War I were necessary to prepare the world for closing time?

6
WORLD WAR I –
THREAT TO SURVIVAL

While traveling on a train the West, Leon Tucker spoke to a Jew about Israel. The Jew said he was perfectly satisfied in the United States. His home was here, his business was here, and his family had become established here. He was not interested in Jerusalem of the building of the nation of Israel.

"Stretch out your right hand," Tucker said. The Jew held out his right hand and Tucker looked at it. Then he said, "Stick out your tongue, please."

"Are you trying to make a fool of me?" the Jew asked.

"No," Tucker replied, "but I would like to see your tongue." The Jew stuck out his tongue.

Tucker looked at it and quoted from Psalm 137:5,6: *"If I forget thee, O Jerusalem, let my right hand forget her cunning. If I do not remember thee, let my tongue cleave to the roof of my mouth; if I prefer not Jerusalem above my chief joy."*

The Jew bowed his head and with tears said, "I have never been so rebuked in my life." [1]

The Young Idealists

The years following the founding of Zionism demonstrated that many Jews had indeed forgotten Jerusalem. Having become comfortable, especially in the West, most Jews preferred to stay in the nations to which they had wandered.

Just before the turn of the century, however, there was a

wave of Jewish immigrants to Palestine. Moved by Herzl's book and his eloquence, a number of young idealists came as pioneers to the land of Abraham, Isaac, and Jacob.

Many of these new arrivals were students. The education they were to receive in their chosen land was to be a difficult one. Palestine was under the control of Turkey, a nation hostile to Jews. The land was denuded of forests and most of it had returned to desert. Ancient terraces that had once protected the soil of Israel had long been destroyed, and erosion had conquered much of the are a. The vital partnership of soil and farmer, so needed for agricultural success, had been broken for centuries and conditions were deplorable.

Mark Twain, who visited Palestine in 1867, described it as:

"...a desolate country whose soil is rich enough, but is given over wholly to weeds—a silent mournful expanse. ...A desolation is here that not even imagination can grace with the pomp of life and action.... We never saw a human being on the whole route.... There was hardly a tree or a shrub anywhere. Even the olive and the cactus, those fast friends of a worthless soil, had almost deserted the country." [2]

Even as late as 1913, the report of the Palestine Royal Commission quotes an eyewitness account of the Maritime Plain as follows:

The road leading from Gaza to the north was only a summer track suitable for transport by camels and carts. ...No orange groves, orchards or vineyards were to be seen until one reached Yabna village.... Not in a single village in all this area was water used for irrigation.... Houses were all of mud. No windows were anywhere to be seen.... The ploughs used were of wood.... The yields were very poor.... The sanitary conditions in the village were horrible. Schools did not exist.... The rate of infant mortality was very high.... The western part, towards the sea, was almost a desert.... The villages in this area were few and thinly populated. Many ruins of villages were scattered over the area, as owing to the prevalence of malaria; many villages were deserted by their inhabitants. [3]

But this hostile land would be tamed. The desert would yet blossom as the rose.

As the years passed, trained people would arrive—scientific farmers, irrigation experts, builders of factories and cities, educators, and thinkers. These immigrants of diverse abilities and interests would in the next three- quarters of a century bring the dead land to life a gain. But what a task lay before them!

By 1914 there were about 100,000 Jews in Palestine, mostly in the area of Jerusalem. Though Herzl was no longer living, his dream was beginning to materialize. Foundations were being laid. Preparations were being made for the birth of a nation. Then World War I broke out.

Caught in the Middle

World conflict was especially unwanted by the Jews. Being small in number and finding themselves caught in the middle of strategic territory held by Turkey and desired by Great Britain, many Jews feared the worst—death of their nation before its birth, the abortion of Israel, the destruction of Zionism.

Turkey's alliance with Germany threatened disaster to Jews in Palestine. Work had to be halted on the homeland. Jews with citizenship in any of the Allied nations were deported. Some Jews were forced to accept Turkish citizenship. Dozens were executed, accused of spying for the Allies.

Another problem for Jews in World War I was a division of loyalties. Jews fought on both sides of the conflict, and with equal patriotism. Unlike World War II, when Germany was an enemy of all Jewish people and thus unified them, World War I offered no such clear-cut decision. Jews in Germany were generally loyal to that land and served with devotion.

War Does Not Take God by Surprise

Although World War I brought great difficulties to the Jews and made the development of their homeland precarious, there were some important positive results from that tragic conflict. Students of the Bible understand that all events work out God's great plan. Even war does not take God by surprise. The working out of His program is not affected by the violence of man: "*Surely the wrath of man shall praise thee: the remainder of wrath shalt thou restrain*" (Ps. 76:10).

The first positive spin-off from World War I was the issuing of what is known as t he Balfour Declaration. Eager to involve the Jews on the side of the Allies and being especially concerned about their strategic location near the Suez Canal, British foreign secretary Arthur James Balfour, on November 2, 1917, sent the following declaration to Lord Rothschild expressing British sympathy with the cause of Zionism:

"His Majesty's Government views with favor the establishment in Palestine of a national home for the Jewish people, and will use their best endeavors to facilitate the achievement of this object, it being clearly understood that nothing shall be done which may prejudice the civil and religious rights of existing non-Jewish communities in Palestine or the rights and political status enjoyed by Jews in any other country."

British support for the establishment of the State of Israel was now on paper and declared to the world. If the aim of that move was to gain Jewish participation in the war, it was successful. The publication of the Balfour Declaration produced Jewish volunteers for service from Great Britain and other nations, especially the United States. It appeared now that instead of destroying Zionism, as had been feared, World War I would actually play an important role in establishing the Jews in their land.

Freedom for Jerusalem!

The second important development in the wartime drama was the arrival there of British General Allenby. The conquest of Jerusalem became one of his first objectives, and the success of his effort is well known.

The Balfour Declaration had been issued on November 2, 1917. One month later, General Allenby freed Jerusalem from the Turks. On December 9, 1917, Allenby's forces liberated Jerusalem without firing a shot. When the Turks had discovered that a general was on the way whose name was Allenby (to them "Allah Bey"—the Prophet of God), they had taken this to mean God was against them and they evacuated the city. It is also said that seeing airplanes in battle for the first time panicked the Turks because they were aware of Isaiah's promise of Jerusalem's deliverance: "*As birds flying, so will the LORD of hosts defend Jerusalem; defending also he will deliver it; and passing over he will preserve it*" (Isaiah 31:5).

Whatever the reasons, Jerusalem was free and the Jews rejoiced. And what a great occasion that victory must have been for General Allenby! He later told how as a boy as he knelt to say his evening prayers he had been taught by his mother to pray: "And 0, Lord, we would not forget thine ancient people, Israel. Hasten the day when Israel shall again be Thy people and shall be restored to Thy favor and to their land." At a reception given for him in London, Allenby said, "I never knew that God would give me the privilege of helping to answer my own childhood prayers."[4]

Statehood for Israel

A third benefit resulting from World War I was the public and official appreciation given to Dr. Chaim Weizmann, a Jew, for his contribution to the war effort of the Allies. Weizmann, who was born in Russia in 1874, studied chemistry in Germany and then taught at universities in Switzerland and England. During World War I he devised an improved method of making acetone, which is used in making explosives. This discovery may actually have affected the outcome of the war.

The prime minister of England credited Weizmann with saving the British army because of his work in providing explosives. When Great Britain tried to reward Weizmann for his work, he said, "There is nothing I want for myself, but there is something I would like you to do for my people." Weizmann requested the establishment in Palestine of a national homeland. It was generally thought that his work had a great deal to do with bringing about the Balfour Declaration. Weizmann later became the first president of the State of Israel.

Following the war, the newly formed League of Nations approved the providing of a national homeland for the Jews as outlined by the Balfour Resolution. President Woodrow Wilson proposed that the land of Palestine be under a British mandate as a temporary arrangement, the ultimate aim being emancipation and independence of that area. The proposal was adopted and the Jews rejoiced.

All seemed ready now for the fulfilling of the words of the Hebrew prophets concerning the return of the Jewish people to their land:

> *For thus saith the Lord God; Behold, I, even I, will both search my sheep, and seek them out. As a shepherd seeketh out his flock in the day that he is among his sheep that are scattered; so will I seek out my sheep, and w ill deliver them out of all places*

where they have been scattered in the cloudy and dark day. And I will bring them out from the people, and gather them from the countries, and will bring them to their own land, and feed them upon the mountains of Israel by the rivers, and in all the inhabited places of the country. I will feed them in a good pasture, and upon the high mountains of Israel shall their fold be: there shall they lie in a good fold, and in a fat pasture shall they feed upon the mountains of Israel. I will feed my flock, and I will cause them to lie down, saith the Lord God (Ezekiel 34:11-15).

But the battle was far from won. Difficult days were ahead for the Jews. The British mandate in Palestine did not turn out as the Zionists had hoped. Disappointment lingered. The vision of hundreds of thousands of Jews pouring into Palestine would have to wait another generation for fulfillment. Frustrating quotas allowing only small numbers of Jewish immigrants plagued the planners of this new nation. The struggle continued.

But What of the Arabs?

Hoping to keep peace with the Arabs, the British placed ridiculously small immigration quotas on the Jews. In 1930, a Royal Commission of Inquiry under agricultural and settlement expert Sir John Hope Simpson concluded that only 20,000 more settlers could be admitted to the land without forcing the Arabs out. At that time there were approximately 850,000 Arabs and 170,000 Jews living there. Simpson could not foresee that in the years to come millions would occupy the area, enjoying a far higher standard of living then he observed in 1930.

To support their restrictions of Jewish immigration, the British issued a series of "white papers" that supposedly gave good reasons for their action. The most shocking of the policies set forth in these official documents was the declaration that within a specified time a majority vote of the Arabs could halt all Jewish immigration. Of the final of these infamous papers, Winston Churchill said:

> "There is much in this white paper which is alien to the spirit of the Balfour Declaration, but I will not trouble about that. I will select the one point upon which there is plainly a breach and repudiation of the Balfour Declaration, the decision that Jewish immigration can be stopped in five years time by an Arab majority. This is a plain breach of a solemn obligation."[5]

Others joined Churchill in protesting the injustice, but the British continued their restrictive action throughout their mandate. It would take another global war to finally build Jewish resolution sufficient to break down the barriers that made it illegal for them to reenter the land.

Winning the War but Losing the Peace

Hindsight declares that in World War I the Allies won the war but lost the peace. One of the reasons for this tragedy was the bitterness born in a young Austrian corporal in the German army named Adolf Hitler.

Angered at the humiliation brought to his people by the Treaty of Versailles that ended World War I and bitter about society in general, Hitler set out to get revenge. He found a sympathetic following among many of the veterans of the defeated German army and later, in the economic chaos that befell Germany, among a good portion of the population. His ultimate political success, making him dictator of Germany, became one of the most regrettable developments of the twentieth century.

Though volumes have been written attempting to analyze the troubled mind of Adolf Hitler, his hatred of the Jews found expression in such inhuman policies and practices that they can only be attributed to satanic influence.

Taking the reins of the German government, he would embark on a binge of bloodshed that would victimize all nations. But none would suffer as the Jews. Six million of the children of Israel would die at the hands of Hitler and his henchmen. The world would never be the same again, and Jews everywhere would be determined to settle for nothing less than a land of their own—the land of their fathers.

7
HITLER'S HOLOCAUST–
THE TRAVAIL OF ISRAEL

The Jews have enriched all the nations in which they have settled—an inevitable fact because of the promise given to Abraham when he left his home to go to a land of God's choosing: *"And I will make of thee a great nation, and I will bless thee, and make thy name great, and thou shalt be a blessing"* (Gen. 12:2).

According to the psalmist, God chose Israel for His "peculiar treasure" (Ps. 135:4). And although it has not often been recognized, the Jews have been a treasure to all nations of the world.

Mark Twain wrote:

"Jews constitute but one percent of the human race. It suggests a nebulous, dim puff of stardust in the blaze of the Milky Way. Properly the Jew ought hardly to be heard of, but he is heard of. He is as prominent on this planet as any other people. His commercial importance is extravagantly out of proportion to the smallness of his bulk. His contributions to the world's list of great names in literature, science, art, music, finance, medicine, and abstruse learning are also altogether out of proportion to the weakness of his numbers. He has made a marvelous fight in the world in all the ages and he has done it with his hands tied behind him." [1]

Blessings through the Jews

Even those who hate Jews take advantage daily of their many contributions. Those who have heart disease and use digitalis are benefiting from the work of Ludwig Traube. If one has a tooth-ache and uses Novocain, he is helped by the work of Carl Koller. If one contacts typhoid fever, his recovery is likely to be the result of the work of two Jews, Widal and Weil. If one has diabetes and uses insulin, it is because that product is available through the research work of a Jew named Minkowsky. The list is long; the blessings that come to us through the Jews are many.

When settling in their ancient homeland, the Jews brought blessing to the Arabs who dwelt there. That may sound absurd in the light of present conflicts in the Middle East, but it is true.

In 1937 the Peel Commission was sent by Great Britain to survey the situation in Palestine. The commission was headed by Lord Peel and composed of a group of men of exceptional ability. Its report in part was as follows:

> "It is difficult to detect any deterioration in the condition of the Arab upper class. Landowners have sold substantial pieces of land at a figure far above the price it would have fetched be fore the First World War [It must be noted that this commission's study was during the depression of the thirties].... In recent transactions, mainly Palestinian Arabs have been concerned and the transactions have all been considerable.... Partly, n o doubt as the result of land sales, the effendi class has been able to make substantial invest-ments of capital.... At least six times more Arab-owned land is now planted with citrus than in 1920.... Some of the capital has been directed to building houses for lease or sale to industrial enterprise.... In the light of these facts, we have no doubt that many Arab landowners have benefited finan-cially from Jewish immigration.... A member of the Arab higher committee admitted to us that nowhere in the world are such uneconomic land prices paid as by the Jews in Palestine.
>
> The general beneficent effect of Jewish immigration on Arab welfare is illumined by the fact that the increase

in Arab population is most marked in urban areas affected by Jewish development.... We are also of the opinion that up till now the Arab cultivator has benefited on the whole from the work of British administration and from the presence of the Jews in the country. Wages have gone up and the standard of living has improved. Jewish example has done much to improve Arab cultivation, especially citrus.

The reclamation and anti-malarial work undertaken by Jewish colonists have benefited all Arabs in the neighborhood. Institutions founded with Jewish funds primarily to serve the national home have also served the Arab population. The Arab charge that the Jews have obtained too large a proportion of good land cannot be maintained. Much of the land now carrying orange grove s was sand dunes and swamp when it was purchased." [2]

But if this is true, why the Arab-Israeli conflict?

A similar question might also be asked concerning the reaction to Jews all over the world. Why are the Jews so maligned and hated when they are so productive and helpful? There can be but one explanation—the fulfillment of prophecy: "*And thou shalt become an astonishment, a proverb, and a byword, among all nations whither the Lord shall lead thee*" (Deut. 28:37).

The Dilemma

So the Jew finds himself in a difficult situation. He is a blessing, yet a byword. He is a treasure, yet he experiences great trouble. He is a contributor, yet he causes conflict wherever he goes. In short, although the material gains brought by Jews are desired, the Jew himself is unwanted. Nowhere was this more true than in Germany during the Third Reich. The official government policy became the extermination of the Jews while salvaging their accumulated wealth, including all personal possessions down to the fillings in their teeth.

Hitler's Nazis made no secret of their hatred of the Jews from the very beginning. Part of their platform in 1920 was: "None but members of the nation may be citizens of the state. None but those of German blood, whatever their creed, may be members of the nation. No Jew, therefore, may be a member of the nation." [3]

The Persecution

When Hitler finally came to power in Germany, the fate of the Jews in Europe was sealed. Like many before and after him, Hitler blamed the Jews for all the ills of society. He saw the Treaty of Versailles that ended the First World War as a Jewish document. Weaknesses in the German economy were attributed to the Jews. He faulted the Jews for the birth and presence of communism in the world. He accused the Jews of being revolutionary and instigating internationalism, a supposed plot o f the Jews to destroy Germany and seize control of the world. They became his favorite scapegoat, and their suffering at his hands rivals the most gruesome of human crimes.

Hitler's persecution of the Jews began in 1933; shortly after he took office. On April 7 of that year he stripped all Jews of offices in the German civil service. Government officials, doctors, lawyers, and workers in educational and cultural fields were all required to sign the following statement:

> "I declare officially herewith I do not know of any circumstance—despite careful scrutiny—that may justify the presumption that I am not of Aryan descent; in particular, none of my paternal or maternal parents or grandparents was at any time of the Jewish faith. I am fully aware of the fact that I expose myself to prosecution and dismissal if this declaration proves untrue." [4]

Within three months, thirty thousand heads of Jewish families had been deprived of income.

The future sufferings of the Jews were also announced in two lines of a song called "The Horst Wessel Song," which became the theme of every major parade in Germany. Translated, two lines of the song were: "When Jewish blood flows from the knife, Things will go much better."

Under Hitler's direction there was a steady rise in outrageous demands and unlawful acts against all Jews. By 1938 every synagogue in the nation had been burned, the windows of every Jewish establishment had been shattered, and twenty-five thousand innocent Jews were in concentration camps.

In the infamous Buchenwald camp Jews were shipped and tortured during the day, while throughout the night a voice shouted over the loudspeakers, "Any Jew who wishes to hang himself is asked first to put a piece of paper in his mouth with his number on it so that we may know who he is."

Nazi atrocities against the Jews began to stir world opinion. Finally, in July of 1938, a conference of thirty-two nations was called in order to consider some means of rescue for these persecuted people. Spokesmen for various Jewish groups were heard, including Golda Meir, and the sufferings of the Jews in Germany for the previous five years were reviewed, as well as the evident course of persecution in the future.

Hitler was bent on raising a generation of Jew-haters. Proof of this was demonstrated by the following statement from one of the new German school reading books: "Remember that the Jews are children of the devil and murderers of mankind. Whoever is a murderer deserves to be killed himself." [5] That look at the direction of education in Hitler's Germany ought to have been enough to move the conference to positive action.

But the world united to trap the Jews for Hitler.

A tragic provision was passed on the final day of the conference that closed the door to freedom for the Jews in Germany and most of Europe. The measure read: "The delegates of the countries of asylum are not willing to undertake any obligations toward financing involuntary immigration." [6] In other words, only Jews who could pay their own way would be able to escape. Since Hitler forbade Jews to leave the country with more than five dollars, that resolution made escape impossible.

The action of the conference was so negative that it not only closed the door to freedom for Jews but also closed the mouths of critics in other nations. Hitler reacted to the decision of the conference in a speech, stating: "The other world is oozing sympathy for the poor tormented people but remains hard and obdurate when it comes to helping them." [7]

He informed the South African defense minister: "We shall solve the Jewish problem in the immediate future... the Jews will disappear." [8]

Shortly thereafter, the official newspaper of the Gestapo declared, "Because it is necessary, because we no longer hear the world's screeching, and because after all no power on earth can hinder us, we will now bring the Jewish question to its totalitarian solution." [9]

World War II was especially historic to Jews because it was the first time world Jewry found themselves fighting a common enemy since they had battled the Romans in the first century. In other wars they had patriotically defended the nations in which they had made their homes. Now, recognizing that Hitler was their declared foe, Jews everywhere gave full effort to defeating him.

In 1939, when England declared war on Germany, 130,000 of the 450,000 Jews in Palestine volunteered for combat service with Britain. Jews performed valiantly during the war, both behind enemy lines, where they were in double jeopardy as Jews and freedom fighters and in conventional warfare as part of the armed forces of the Allied nations.

While devotedly serving the Allies, however, the Jews found themselves in a conflicting situation. Hundreds of thousands of

Jews were fleeing before the advancing German army, hoping for entry into Palestine. Incredibly, the doors to that land were closed to them because of Britain's strict immigration policies. Nevertheless, the Jews gave hand and heart to the war effort, fighting as if the hated white paper that barred entrance to their homeland did not exist.

It is doubtful that any people ever suffered as did the Jews during World War II when they were the special object of Hitler's hatred. As the pace of the war increased, so did the mad dictator's effort to destroy the Jews. When German military successes increased Nazi-controlled territory, the noose around Jewish necks was drawn tighter. And the conquest of adjacent nations meant the encirclement of hundreds of thousands more of the Jews in Europe, who then became raw materials for Hitler's death factories, targets for his Jew-killing machine.

Moses had written:

Because thou servedst not the Lord thy God with joyfulness, and with gladness of heart, for the abundance of all things; Therefore shalt thou serve thine enemies which the LORD shall send against thee, in hunger, and in thirst, and in nakedness, and in want of all things: and he shall put a yoke of iron upon thy neck, until he have destroyed thee (Deut. 28:47, 48).

Hunger, thirst, and nakedness were only part of the privations and persecutions experienced by the Jews within Hitler's reach. German technical genius was set to work to build efficient equipment for the total destruction of the Jews. In Hitler's words, this was to be the "final solution" to the Jewish problem.

The Murder Missions

When the German army moved into Russia, mobile killing units were dispatched for the sole purpose of following the army and killing Jews. Within five months, these murder missions had brought death to 500,000 Jews. Ultimately, about one and one-half million of the children of Israel would fall before the bullets of the Einsatsgruppen (the mobile killing units).

Equally dangerous to Jews were the mobile gas vans which were first used in Kelmo, Poland. Ninety Jews at a time were packed into each van and asphyxiated by carbon monoxide. The death rate in this operation ran about one thousand Jews per day.

But without doubt, the most efficient Jew killers were the Nazi concentration camps or "death factories." And there were many: Westerbork, Vught, Bergen-belsen, Buchenwald, Dachau, Grossrosen, Mauthausen, Ebensee, Theresienstadt, Sobibor, Auschwitz, Treblinka, and others.

Like a great industrial complex stretching across the ever-enlarging German empire, the camps were fed by trainloads of raw materials—Jews—and expected to produce whatever would pro fit the Third Reich. Hundreds of thousands of Jews were loaded into cattle cars and shipped like animals to the camps to be processed through the gas chambers and ovens.

The story is almost too hideous to tell. Moses had written, *"Thy life shall hang in doubt before thee..."* (Deut. 28:66) and the prophecy was literally fulfilled in the concentration camps of Hitler's "final solution."

Auschwitz was equipped to execute 10,000 Jews per day. Treblinka could destroy 25,000 per day. Arriving at one of these nightmare stations, a Jew might have life or death determined by the whim of one army officer. As the refugees came off the trains, one man might stand motioning to either the right or left. The left could mean the gas chambers while the right might allow a little time to work around the camp before the end.

Death Camp Deception

Reflection on the deception of the death camps is chilling. At Sobibor, a cordial greeting was given to new arrivals. Guards took children on their laps and gave them goodies. They were helpful with baggage, making official reports and providing tables for writing letters to friends. Pens and paper completed the illusion of helpfulness.

All the trappings of a holiday resort were at Sobibor. Everything seemed to inspire hope. There were canteens and parks. Rose gardens decorated the grounds. Yet it was there that in March of 1943 a wild celebration followed the execution of the millionth Jew. There was no hope at Sobibor.

Treblinka was set up as a rest center, a sanatorium. There was a waiting room and a railroad ticket office, giving the illusion that one would be able to buy his ticket for return after an assigned time there. Yet there was no return. Those arriving at Treblinka had simply entered the hopper of another of Hitler's killing machines. They would be destroyed, becoming some of the six million who were victims of Nazi hatred of the Jewish people.

The cooperation of non-Nazis in shipping Jews to their death is an unhappy story. Dutch resistance fighter J. A. Scheps rebuked his countrymen for their part in this awful slaughter, saying, "Don't you understand what they're doing to these helpless Jews? Don't you know how they torture our Jewish comrades? Have you bread-and-butter patriots never heard the voice of Rachel, she who mourns and will not be comforted for her children, the children you help carry to their death?" [10]

Scheps challenged the Dutch engineers to refuse to carry the cattle cars full of Jews to their deaths. He called upon them to take a stand for righteousness and decency. Few did. Dutch trainmen transported 60,000 Dutch Jews in sixty-seven trains to one camp, Auschwitz, and only 500 returned.

The general procedure for Dutch Jews arriving at Auschwitz was to gas them immediately after being unloaded from the train. This was the heartless "It's-time- to-take-a-shower" routine. Usually women and children were taken first. All were ordered to undress in a common room. Clothes had to be neatly folded and shoes tied together (these would be sent to non-Jews thought worthy by the Third Reich).

The gas chamber appeared to be a shower room. To add reality to the lie, those entering were given a piece of soap and were promised a cup of coffee after the shower. When the room was packed with Jews, the forbidding door was shut and the gas was turned on. Within fifteen minutes the gruesome charade was over and it was time for the scavengers to begin their work. Gold teeth were removed. Wedding rings were taken off dead fingers. Women's hair was cut off. And the corpses were shoved into the ovens. The ritual was repeated again and again with the unfeeling efficiency of an assembly line. The end products were ashes and the few remaining possessions of European Jews who had already been robbed and uprooted. [11]

The degree of Nazi hatred for the Jews may have been best expressed by the infamous Adolf Eichmann, who said, "I shall leap laughing into my grave, for the thought that I have five million human lives on my conscience is to me a source of inordinate satisfaction." [12]

Can the fountain from which such thoughts flow be anything but satanic?

As the war drew to its close and Hitler's defeat was imminent, it became clear that history was about to bury another company of Jew-haters. God's promise to Abraham was invulnerable even to the military might of the Third Reich: "*And I will bless them that bless thee, and curse them that curseth thee: and in thee shall all families of the earth be blessed*" (Gen. 12:3).

On November 26, 1945, a statement by a Nazi doctor known for his bitterness toward Jews was published in Nuremberg, Germany. Admitting the tragedy of his own involvement in the attempted destruction of the Jews, he wrote:

"We have forsaken God and therefore were forsaken by

God.... Anti-Semitism distorted our outlook and we made grave errors. It is hard to admit mistakes, but the whole existence of our people is in question. We Nazis must have the courage to rid ourselves of anti-Semitism. We have to declare to the youth that it was a mistake." [13]

And what a mistake it was! It produced untold misery f or the Jews, exterminating six million of them and writing pages of disgrace in history concerning Hitler and the Nazis that will never be forgotten.

How different it might have been!

One author says: "Had Hitler loved the Israelites instead of hating them, he might have averted the greatest of all wars, the greatest of all destruction programs, and engendered the admiration of the world instead of its hatred." [14]

Results of the Slaughter

Hitler's holocaust was decisive in bringing about the birth of the nation of Israel. European Jews had learned a hard lesson. They must never feel at home except in their own homeland.

The population of European Jews in 1939 had been 9,739,200. By 1945, Hitler's death camps and his portable killing units had reduced that population to 3,505,130. More than six million of the children of Israel had been victims of this slaughter.

Nevertheless, the Jews as a people were alive—and Hitler was dead.

There was a future to be shaped, a homeland to be developed and work to be done in the land of their fathers. The Jews would do it. Having survived the holocaust, they were not to be denied t heir homeland. Immigration quotas and all other obstacles would be swept away in a new exodus to the land of Palestine.

The travail was not over. More years of struggle remained. But the birth of a nation was in sight—the long-prophesied birth of the nation of Israel.

Other areas of God's prophetic program were developed by World War II. Russia had emerged as a military power. Europe was a shambles and would sense the need of cooperation and some kind of economic and political union, foreshadowing Daniel's prophecy of the revival of the Roman Empire. The immense wealth of the United States would be drained through postwar rebuilding of other nations and in acting as the world's peace-keeper and defender against communism, preparing the way for a power shift to Europe and the Mediterranean area. China and other nations of the East had been affected by the conflict and would move toward their end-time destinies.

Frightened, the world had entered the perilous nuclear age—announcing the approach of closing time.

8
BIRTHDAY

Ezekiel prophesied the formation of the State of Israel in the last days: *"For I will take you from among the heathen and gather you out of all countries, and will bring you into your own land"* (Ezek. 36:24).

But the long centuries rolled on and the promise was not fulfilled.

Students of prophecy insisted a time would come when the Jews would return to their homeland, and when the Zionist movement began to promote the settlement of Jews in Palestine some had the courage to identify this as the fulfillment of Ezekiel's prophecy.

Others were skeptical. The movement seemed so small and the obstacles to its success appeared to be insurmountable. Propaganda against the Zionists by anti-Semites began to be circulated, associating the movement with a conspiracy to rule the world. It was not popular to be on the side of Jewish pioneers in Palestine.

Aftermath

Nevertheless, the settlement of the Jewish homeland continued. Although hampered by restrictive immigration quotas set by the British during their mandate, the Jews kept pressing forward, counting each new village as another step in the establishment of their long-awaited home. In the difficult years from

1939 to 1947 there were 94 new villages founded, making 349 Jewish settlements in that hostile land.

Hitler's holocaust annihilated two out of every three European Jews, one-third of the entire Jewish race, and uprooted Jews who had become comfortable in their European homes. In their book, *Israel*, David M. Jacobs and Kees Scherer describe the impact of the holocaust as follows:

> "The shock of this terrible disaster finally gave the Jews the power of desperation so that against the logic of history and politics, a mere three years after the greatest catastrophe in their history, came one of their greatest triumphs: on May 15, 1948, the State of Israel was established." [1]

But those three years were difficult ones.

Having given of themselves to the Allied war effort, the Jews had hoped for cooperation from the Allies in establishing their nation.

They were disappointed.

Balancing on the brink of bankruptcy, Great Britain was determined to cling to friendship with the Arabs for economic reasons, not wanting to lose their single most important resource: oil. Some of their pipelines ran through Arab lands and they were not willing to risk the loss of oil for the sake of the Jews. Consequently, the British continued to restrict Jewish immigration following the war.

Burdened by the plight of their countrymen in Europe and frustrated by the restrictive British mandate, the Jews went underground and began to prepare for a fight for freedom. Infiltrating several British military bases, they stole light arms. They also dealt in captured Axis weapons and engaged in pressure tactics designed to ultimately force the British out of their homeland.

In Europe, conditions for Jews remained difficult. Although delivered from Hitler's death camps, they were still in serious trouble. By the end of 1946, more than a quarter of a million displaced Jews were packed into camps in western Germany. As a result, the British loosened immigration restrictions somewhat, but the trickle of immigrants allowed into Palestine was still tiny compared to the tens of thousands waiting in the crowded displaced-persons camps of Europe.

A Modern Exodus

Since they were unable to get realistic concessions from the British, the Jews tackled the problem themselves. Sending Jews from Palestine to infiltrate the displaced-persons camps, they began to organize the refugees and prepare them to enter Palestine under cover. They also took advantage of the poor conditions in the camps to draw world attention to the hardships still faced by European Jews.

Soon a modern exodus was under way from Germany to Palestine. Jews were taken from Germany to the French and Austrian borders, then through mountain passes on foot to the Italian or French coasts. It was a difficult route from Germany to Palestine, but these struggling people had been enroute to that land for nearly two thousand years. They had taken the most crushing blows tyrants could give and had survived. Terrain would not deter them now.

The chaos of postwar Europe cooperated in allowing the Jews to move across Europe to the Mediterranean. In Italy they found the hatred of British occupation working in their favor. This former Axis power now helped the Jews on their homeward trek.

Nearly all the ships that carried Jews from Europe to Palestine were Italian coastal vessels of prewar vintage. Few of these obsolete tubs were fit for the crossing. Nevertheless, they were repaired hastily at Italian shipyards and sent on their precarious voyages.

In Palestine the Jewish underground awaited the arrival of

the immigrants and employed covert methods to smuggle the new arrivals into the country. They were often able to monitor official radio messages and then decoy the British while the refugees landed.

Blockade

The success of the smuggling operation was short-lived. The British intensified their blockade, making it almost impenetrable; and by 1946, 80,000 troops patrolled the country.

Looking back, the scene seems unreal. These survivors of Hitler's holocaust and the crowded camps of Europe were now crossing the Mediterranean in rickety ships only to be met by a mighty British blockade commissioned to keep them from entering the land of their dreams.

Once stopped by the blockade, the Jews were transferred to British transports on which they were taken to Cyprus, where more refugee camps waited. Long before this heartbreaking ordeal Solomon had written, "*Hope deferred maketh the heart sick...*" (Proverbs 13:12). The wise king's observation must have described the experience of thousands of his people who were turned from their homeland after making the long journey to its very borders.

In spite of the blockade, however, the Jewish spirit was not broken. Palestine was still the goal of this persistent people, and they intended to reach it. Their determination was expressed by the immigrants on board the Beauharnais when their ship was towed into Haifa Harbor, having been captured by the British. Its passengers unfurled a long banner over the deck that said: "We survived Hitler. Death is no stranger to us. Nothing can keep us from our Jewish homeland. The blood be on your head if you fire on this unarmed ship."

Records show that all but five of the sixty-three refugee ships were intercepted in efforts to reach Palestine between 1945 and 1948. Estimates of the number of displaced persons confined in the Cyprus camps ranged from 26,000 to 65,000.

In an effort to discourage immigration and attempts to run the blockade, the camps at Cyprus were anything but comfortable. They were extremely hot in the summer, water was generally short, and the food was poor and scarce. In spite of the risk, however, they continued their efforts to enter their land with the force of a battering ram, never relaxing their pressure on the British to allow them to come home.

The Three-Way Struggle

In Palestine a three-way struggle continued between Jews, Arabs, and the British, with the Jews holding tenaciously to each hard-earned village and settlement. The attitude of the massive Arab and British forces about them must have created a situation reminiscent of an earlier return of Jews to their land, when their enemies said: *"What do these feeble Jews? will they fortify themselves? will they sacrifice? will they make an end in a day? will they revive the stones out of the heaps of the rubbish which are burned?"* (Nehemiah 4:2).

Now as then the Jews continued to develop their land in spite of dangers, and to protect themselves as had their forefathers under Nehemiah, who had written:

> *And it came to pass from that time forth, that the half of my servants wrought in the work, and the other half of them held both the spears, the shields, and the bows, and the habergeons; and the rulers were behind all the house of Judah. They which builded on the wall, and they that bare burdens, with those that laded, every one with one of his hands wrought in the work, and with the other hand held a weapon. For the builders, every one had his sword girded by his side, and so builded. And he that sounded the trumpet was by me* (Nehemiah 4:16-18).

U. N. Intervention

The continual struggle in Palestine was finally too much for the British. They were tired of the terrorism, the sabotage, the continual conflict between the Arabs and the Jews, and the expense. On April 2, 1947, Great Britain turned the fate of Palestine over to the United Nations. It was an historic action that would ultimately bring about the establishment of the State of Israel.

On November 29, 1947, after careful investigation, the United Nations voted to partition Palestine, giving independence to the Jews. The partition gave the Jews only about one-fourth of the amount of territory they originally intended for their homeland. It was only ten miles wide at its middle and vulnerable to attack on nearly every side. But to the Jews, the decision for partition meant independence, and they hailed the United Nations' action with joy. At last they would have a home of their own.

Birth of a Nation

The date for statehood was finally set for May 15, 1948. As the occasion approached, Jewish excitement over independence was tempered by the threat of war with the Arabs. Being seriously undermanned and under gunned, they simply were not ready for war. Arms had been brought from Europe, but the British would not allow them to be used until after the mandate had ended. Arab leaders were promising a war of extermination. Having traveled the long trail from Hitler's camps to their homeland, it now appeared that another Nazi-like experience awaited the Jews. But regardless of the danger, the Jews proceeded with preparations for the birth of their nation.

At eight in the morning on May 14, the British lowered the Union Jack in Jerusalem. By mid-afternoon there was a full-scale war on throughout the country between the Arabs and the Jews.

At 4:00 P.M. that day, David Ben-Gurion read the Declaration of Independence of Israel and it was broadcast from the Tel Aviv Museum. He began:

> The land of Israel was the birthplace of the Jewish people.
> Here their spiritual, religious, and national identity was formed. Here they achieved independence and created a culture of national and universal significance. Here they wrote and gave the Bible to the world.
> Exiled from Palestine, the Jewish people remained faithful to it in all the countries of their dispersion, never ceasing to pray and hope for their return and restoration of their national freedom.

Concluding the Declaration, Ben-Gurion said:

> In the midst of wanton aggression, we call upon the Arab inhabitants of the State of Israel to return to the ways of peace and play their part in the development of the State with full and equal citizenship and due representation in all its bodies and institutions—provisional or permanent.
> We offer peace and unity to all the neighboring states and their peoples, and invite them to cooperate with the independent Jewish nation for the common good of all.
> Our call goes out to the Jewish people all over the world to rally to our side in the task of immigration and development and to stand by us in the great struggle for the fulfillment of the dream of generations—the redemption of Israel. [For the full text of the Israeli Declaration of Independence, see the Appendix.]

The United States was the first country to recognize the State of Israel, with President Truman's statement of recognition coming at 6:10 P.M. on May 14.

On that day, the following editorial appeared in the *New York Times:*

"This is the last day of British rule in Palestine. At midnight (6:00 this afternoon our time), Great Britain surrenders the mandate which she received from the League of Nations twenty-five years ago. The zero hour, awaited with hope and anxiety by the bitterly divided population, marks a fateful change in the status and government of a small country that has presented the United Nations with its hardest test to date and weighs more heavily than any other on the heart and conscience of the world.

Palestine will now be an independent entity for the first time in centuries." [2]

The long-awaited statehood had arrived. Israel was born.

The War of Independence

On May 15, from Tel Aviv at 5:25 in the morning, Ben-Gurion was broadcasting Israel's thanks to the United States for prompt recognition of their statehood. A loud explosion interrupted his speech. After a pause, he said, "A bomb has just fallen on this city from enemy aircraft flying overhead." The War of Independence had begun.

To call it the "War of Independence" seems a contradiction. Most nations trace their histories to a war of independence after which statehood was won. In Israel's case, the long struggle for statehood was capped by a war of independence. Although there had been sporadic fighting throughout the country in the months preceding the end of the British mandate, the actual war began on the birthday of the nation. Although travail usually accompanies birth, in this historic situation travail and trouble continued after birth had taken place.

The War of Independence was bloody and desperate. Had

the Arabs known how poorly the Jews were armed they might have pressed their advantage and quickly won the war. The Arabs had been able to purchase weapons on the open market because they were recognized nations. Europe was then a giant weapons market, a sort of postwar rummage sale, but the Jews had been hindered in purchasing arms because of their political status. They had been able to secure some World War II arms, but at the beginning of the war they had only four large howitzers of the type used by the French army in the Franco-Prussian war of 1870.

In one battle with forty-five Syrian tanks, only two of the ancient howitzers were available, having been hurriedly moved from Haifa to be used in the defense of the oldest kibbutz in Palestine. Colonel Moshe Dayan, the local commander, ordered his men to fire at the most advanced Syrian tank. The Israelis scored a direct hit, causing the column to turn around and retreat. They never returned. Had the Syrians known they had been fired upon with one of the only two weapons on hand at the time, they would have undoubtedly used their strength and firepower to win the battle.

The Arab League nations that opposed Israel were Egypt, Iraq, Saudi Arabia, Syria, Yemen, Lebanon, and Trans Jordan. They formed a formidable alliance against less than a million poorly armed Jews. Many of the Arabs fought well and Jewish casualties were high. Six thousand Israelis were killed during the eight months of war. Had American losses been that high proportionately during World War II, they would have reached two million, which is more than the number killed in both world wars.

Triumphant in Travail

When in January, 1949, all fighting ended in the War of Independence, the small, ill-armed Jewish militia had developed into a seasoned fighting force supported by armor and fighter planes. Not only had the Jews survived, but they had increased their territory by six hundred miles. The final armistice gained them 21 percent more land than they had originally been given in the U.N. partition. They had been triumphant in their travail, and the world took notice.

Following the birth of the nation, the first official act of the State of Israel had been to set aside the white paper quotas, opening the doors of immigration to Jews everywhere. In the eighteen months following that action, 340,000 Jews arrived in their homeland. They poured in even during the war, and by June 30, 1953, the population had doubled. By the end of fifteen months following statehood, fifty-two displaced-persons' camps in Europe had been closed and all the inhabitants sent to Israel.

The prophesied return to Palestine of the children of Israel was happening. Isaiah had written: *"Fear not: for I am with thee: I will bring thy seed from the east, and gather thee from the west; I will say to the north, Give up; and to the south, Keep not back: bring my sons from far, and my daughters from the ends of the earth"* (Isaiah 43:5,6).

Coming Home

And from all directions they came.

They came from the east. The largest group arriving from the east came from Iraq, the ancient land of Babylon. At the time of the War of Independence, 135,000 Jews lived in Iraq. After the war, when they were allowed to return to Israel, they were required to leave all their wealth behind. It is estimated that they left assets worth five million dollars. Speaking of that exodus, Dr. Weizmann said, "Now we see the end of the Babylonian captivity."

They came from the west. Jews arrived from the west more slowly than from other directions because the largest group of Jews there had settled in the United States. Being comfortable in America, they were not eager to leave. However, the financial resources of American Jews allowed them to invest heavily in founding the national home.

There are more than 5 million Jews in the United States, a number that exceeds the population of Israel (3.5 million) [This was 1979 – as of December 2014 there are 6.2 millions Jews in Israel]. Their success here may have been the blessing of God for the very purpose of enabling them to give financial support to those settling in the State of Israel.

They came from the north. From Hitler's camps and the displaced-persons camps they came. From all the nations of Europe they came. Having learned the lesson of the holocaust, they came to Israel. They came home.

They came from the south. They came from Yemen and other lands south of Israel. The story of the Yemenite Jews and their return is a tale in itself.

Considering themselves exiles in Yemen, the Jews eagerly received the word that the State of Israel had been established and that a new David was in power (David Ben-Gurion, the first prime minister of Israel).

Gathering up what possessions they could carry, great numbers of them started the journey to Israel. When their countrymen in Israel heard of it, an airlift was organized. Converted bombers were prepared to bring the Yemenite Jews home. In his book, *Israel, the Key to Prophecy*, William L. Hull described the scene:

"Large planes, converted bombers, were flown to Aden. They contained only benches running lengthwise in the plane and thus enabling up to 130 of the small undersized sized Yemenite Jews to be loaded into one plane. It was all new to the Yemenites. They were a primitive people and entirely unacquainted with machinery or modern scientific development. Only a handful of all the Jews in Yemen had ever seen a plane before or even an automobile. With considerable trepidation, the crew prepared for the first flight from Aden. What would be the reaction of these primitive people? Thousands were to be transported. The first flight would indicate what might be expected.

Slowly men, women, and children made their way up the steps, took their places on the benches, sitting cross-legged, and waited in wonder. The crew was wondering, too. The roar of the motors, the movement of the plane, the sudden lifting from the ground, any of these could cause a stampede in the plane. A rush to the door, a crowding of all to one side or an attack upon the crew might wreck the plane. But nothing did happen. Everyone sat quietly, open-mouthed, breathless. Then the plane moved off and was airborne. Soon it was flying smoothly with its strange human cargo. The Yemenites just smiled and explained that God has promised that "they shall mount up with wings as eagles." Here were the eagle's wings provided to bring them back to Zion. Surely it was time for the Messiah to come. Maybe He awaited them in Israel!

All together 48,000 Jews were flown to Israel from Yemen."[3]

The Jews, a people noted for their business ability, made a total investment in the State of Israel. They came burning their bridges behind them. Sometimes they were required to leave the labor of a lifetime to start anew as pioneers in a new land.

And yet this land was not new! Something within had called them back to the land of their fathers. At last the Jews were coming home.

9
HOME TO STAY?

Bruised and bleeding from centuries of suffering, the Jews came home to the land of their fathers. They bought their ancient land at premium prices from its Arab owners, fulfilling the words of their prophets:

> *For thus saith the LORD; Like as I have brought all this great evil upon this people, so will I bring upon them all the good that I have promised them. And fields s hall be bought in this land, whereof ye say, It is desolate without man or beast; it is given into the hand of the Chaldeans. Men shall buy fields for money, and subscribe evidences, and seal them, and take witnesses in the land of Benjamin, and in the places about Jerusalem, and in the cities of Judah, and in the cities of the mountains, and in the cities of the valley, and in the cities of the south: for I will cause their captivity to return, saith the Lord* (Jeremiah 32:42-44).

Paying the Price

But in bringing about the birth of their nation, the Jews also had to pay the price of blood. Desiring to retrieve the land they had sold, the Arabs battled the Jews for decades. And after the nation's birth, the struggle continued still.

Considering the odds for survival in a conflict with the Arabs, some Jews wondered whether they had bought a beach-head or established a nation. Their tiny land hardly compared in

97

size with its neighbors, and the population of 650,000 at the time of the nation's birth seemed minute compared to that of the Arab nations surrounding them (approximately fifty million). Still, the promises of scattering and persecution had been fulfilled, so why not the promises of restoration and blessing? Size or strength of opponents certainly did not alter the promises of God:

> *Therefore all they that devour thee shall be devoured; and all thine adversaries, every one of them, shall go into captivity; and they that spoil thee shall be a spoil, and all that prey upon thee will I give for a prey. For I will restore health unto thee, and I will heal the e of thy wounds, saith the Lord; because they called thee an Outcast, saying, This is Zion, whom no man seeketh after* (Jeremiah 30:16,17).

Although the Jews began their return to Palestine in unbelief, still not having accepted their Messiah, they did cling to the biblical promises concerning their land. In 1956, when they again found themselves fighting for their lives, Radio Jerusalem broadcasted the words of the prophet Amos:

> *And I will bring again the captivity of my people of Israel, and they shall build the waste cities, and inhabit them; and they shall plant vineyards, and drink the wine thereof; they shall also make gardens, and eat the fruit of them. And I will plant them upon their land, and they shall no more be pulled up out of their land which I have given them, saith the Lord thy God* (Amos 9:14,15).

Victory came easily in 1956. Israel quickly conquered the Gaza Strip and the major powers intervened to bring about a cease-fire in order to save Egypt from complete collapse.

Between 1956 and 1967, tensions continued to mount. Egypt's President Gamel Abdel Nasser, the leader of the Arab world, boasted of his intention to destroy Israel completely—to push her into the sea and annihilate her citizens.

On May 15, 1967, the anniversary of Israel's independence, Egyptian forces moved into the Sinai. On May 17, Cairo Radio's Voice of the Arabs proclaimed: "All Egypt is now prepared to plunge into total war which will put an end to Israel." [1]

Following the movement of his troops into the Sinai, Nasser demanded the removal of the United Nations Peacekeeping Force stationed there, and on May 18 the Voice of the Arabs announced: "As of today, there no longer exists an international emergency force to protect Israel. The sole method we shall apply against Israel is a total war which will result in the extermination of Zionist existence." [2]

Hoping to exploit the dangerous situation in the Middle East, the Russians sent exaggerated accounts to both Syria and Egypt of the movements of Israeli troops and war materials along their borders. Through these inflated announcements they were successful in fanning the flames of patriotic passion and fear among the Arabs. On May 28, Nasser declared, "We will not accept any co-existence with Israel. Today the issue is not the establishment of peace between the Arab states and Israel. The war is in effect since 1948." [3]

On May 30, he announced, "The armies of Egypt, Jordan, Syria, and Lebanon are poise d on the borders of Israel to face the challenge, while standing behind us are the armies of Iraq, Algeria, Kuwait, Sudan, and the whole Arab nation [all Arabs]. This act will astound the world. Today they will know that the Arabs are arranged for battle. The critical hour has arrived. We have reached the stage of serious action and not declarations." [4]

The Six-Day War of 1967

In an overt act of war, Nasser then closed the crucial Israeli port of Eilat on the Gulf of Aqaba.

The war was on.

The Jews had heard and seen enough, and on June 5 Israeli jets struck a death blow to the Egyptian air force. Israeli tanks rolled into the Sinai. Fierce battles took place in the Golan Heights and in Jerusalem. Russia warned the world to keep hands off, expecting a quick Arab victory. But the dry bones of Ezekiel's vision had begun to come together, and nothing in the prophecy gave any hint of annihilation or a return to the graves of other nations from which they had come. The Jews would not be destroyed, for God had promised to preserve them.

Within six days the Arab forces were in serious retreat. Israeli soldiers had captured the Sinai and the Golan Heights, and Russia was demanding peace in the Middle East. It is significant that Israel had captured all of Jerusalem. All of this ancient and beloved city was in Jewish hands for the first time since A.D. 70, causing Bible students to take a fresh look at Luke 21:24: *"And they shall fall by the edge of the sword, and shall be led away captive into all nations: and Jerusalem shall be trodden down of the Gentiles, until the times of the Gentiles be fulfilled."*

The Six-Day War of 1967 gained world respect for Israel as a military power. Friends of Israel who had feared for her safety now respected her ability to defend herself. The Russians were appalled at their loss of three billion dollars' worth of military aid to the Arabs in a six-day period. Nasser was humiliated; in an attempt to save face he manufactured stories of American and British intervention on the side of Israel.

Israeli soldiers had distinguished themselves as fighting men. Against overwhelming numbers and immense firepower, they had been victorious. The whole experience was reminiscent of Gideon's successful campaign against the Midianites when greatly outnumbered, or of Joshua's conquest of the land of Canaan.

It is clear that God protected His ancient people. But this raises questions: If the scattering of the Jews resulted from their rejection of Christ, why has God brought them back to the land?

Why have the Jews been allowed to return to their land in unbelief ? Why has God protected the people of Israel when they have not received His Son?

The answer to all these questions is simply that God promised through His prophets that in the end time He would bring the Jewish people back into their land, though still in unbelief, but that after arriving there they would turn to Him:

> *Therefore prophesy and say unto them, Thus saith the Lord God; Behold, O my people, I will open your graves, and cause you to come up out of your graves, and bring you into the land of Israel. And ye shall know that I am the LORD, when I have opened your graves, O my people, and brought you up out of your graves, And shall put my spirit in you, and ye shall live, and I shall place you in your own land:* **then** *shall ye know that I the Lord have spoken it, and performed it, saith the Lord* (Ezek. 37:12-14, emphasis mine).

The War of 1973

The war of 1973, or the Yom Kippur War, began on October 6. Most Jews were in their synagogues observing Yom Kippur. Egypt attacked the Sinai Peninsula and Syria attacked the Golan Heights. Eleven Arab nations sent personnel and equipment against Israel. Once again the Jews had their backs to the wall.

Having taken the first blow in the Yom Kippur War, Israeli military forces suffered severe casualties. Within a few days, however, the Jews were on the offensive and the tide of battle was turning in Israel's favor.

The fierce battle of the Golan Heights ended with the Jews conquering all strategic positions there and threatening Damascus. On the Egyptian front, Israeli soldiers crossed the Suez Canal and headed for Cairo. They were in a position to cut off the Egyptian Third Army that had ventured into the Sinai;

had that been done, the Israeli air force would have been able to destroy the Egyptian force without fear of the missiles positioned along the canal. With the two major Arab nations in deep trouble, Russia again demanded peace.

Eager to avoid a major confrontation, the other great powers also brought pressure upon the Jews and Arabs to cease fighting. Once again tiny Israel had successfully defended herself.

Although the Arabs lost the 1973 war to Israel, they did make certain gains. Their fighting was greatly improved and their soldiers more disciplined. At the end of the war the Arabs were far more united than in the past. This new Arab unity brought about the use of a new weapon, perhaps the most deadly that has yet been used against Israel. That weapon is oil.

10
BUT THERE IS NO PEACE

Jerusalem means "city of peace" or "foundation of peace."

But the history of Jerusalem is one of war and destruction.

The sounds of battle, the clash of arms, have been heard in Jerusalem through the centuries. From the siege of David in 1000 B.C. to the Six-Day War of 1967, the city of peace has experienced forty-six sieges and thirty-two partial destructions. It has been burned to the ground five times, yet has always risen from the ashes. It has been the scene of four wars in the past twenty-five years. Today it is the site of the most volatile political, religious, and military problem in the entire world.

The Jewish cry for peace in Jerusalem is sincere, finding its roots in the promise of peace for the Jews given through Moses: *"And I will give peace in the land, and ye shall lie down, and none shall make you afraid: and I will rid evil beasts out of the land, neither shall the sword go through your land"* (Lev. 26:6).

The Jews were instructed to pray for the peace of Jerusalem:

> *Pray for the peace of Jerusalem: they shall prosper that love thee. Peace be within thy walls, and prosperity within thy palaces. For my brethren and companions' sakes, I will now say, Peace be within thee* (Ps. 122:6-8).

> *As for such as turn aside unto their crooked ways, the LORD shall lead them forth with the workers of iniquity: but peace shall be upon Israel* (Ps. 125:5).

Yea, thou shalt see thy children's children, and peace upon Israel (Ps. 128:6).

He maketh peace in thy borders, and filleth thee with the finest of the wheat (Ps. 147:14).

The Jewish desire for peace has waited long and weathered many storms. Since the dispersion, this troubled people has anticipated a day of peace.

Following the Golden Age of Spanish Jewry, during the Spanish Inquisition, while Crusaders attacked them in the Rhine Valley and murdered them in the name of God, the Jews longed for peace.

Suffering unbelievably at the hands of the Cossacks during the Polish rebellion, under the reign of the merciless Czars who instituted the bloody pogroms, the Jews cried for peace.

During Hitler's holocaust, when total annihilation of the Jews in Europe seemed imminent, the Jews longed for peace.

At the birth of their nation in 1948, the Jews longed for peace.

When surrounded by hostile neighbors and under the threat of being pushed into the sea and destroyed by the forces of Nasser in 1967, the Jews longed for peace.

But peace did not come. The long struggle for the end of hostilities continued. Tranquility evaded them. And the words of the prophet Jeremiah seemed to describe their daily experience:

"We looked for peace, but no good came; and for a time of health, and behold trouble!" (Jeremiah 8:15).

The Push for Peace

Today the entire world has a stake in the peace of Jerusalem. As never before, the Middle East is the proverbial powder keg of the world. Informed people everywhere know that a spark of conflict there might ignite a fire that would engulf the entire planet, plunging all of civilization into a nuclear nightmare.

"Pray for the peace of Jerusalem" is good advice for all people.

Talk of peace will be increasingly the order of the day. Western nations, the United Nations, and the Communist world, acting together and unilaterally, may be involved in seeking to both calm and exploit Middle East tensions. Top-notch diplomats will be employed. Peace conferences will be scheduled in the most desirable locations. Behind-the-scenes bargaining between all powers can be expected. Diplomatic arm-twisting will not be overlooked. News releases reporting the slightest progress toward peace will be fed to the public. The push for peace will seem almost irresistible.

But peace will not come easily to the Middle East. Differences there are deep and longstanding. Jerusalem itself presents an almost insurmountable obstacle to peace. It is important to the three major religions of the world: Judaism, Christianity, and Islam. Some Arab leaders are determined to wrest control of Jerusalem from Israel. And the Jews, having finally retaken their most important city, are determined not to give it up.

Jerusalem has passed from one Gentile power to another since 400 B.C. Consider the conquerors since A.D. 70 alone: A.D. 70, the Romans; 614, the Persians; 637, Caliph Omar; 1099, the Crusaders; 1187, Salidan; 1250, the Egyptian Mamalukes; 1517, the Turks; 1917, the British; and finally in our lifetime, 1967, the Jews captured Jerusalem. Zechariah 12:2 - 3 states:

> *Behold I will make Jerusalem a cup of trembling unto all the people round about, when they shall be in the siege both against Judah and against Jerusalem. And in that day will I make Jerusalem a burdensome stone for all people: all that burden themselves with it shall be cut in pieces, though all the people of the earth be gathered together against it.*

An anguished and heartfelt cry for peace is both desirable and dangerous.

The desire shows the heart is right regarding peace, for that is to be the aim of the child of God: *"Depart from evil, and do good; seek peace, and pursue it"* (Ps. 34:14).

On the other hand, one may be so enamored with the hope for peace that he closes his eyes to the danger of accepting fraudulent conditions for peace. Prime Minister C. Neville Chamberlain of England met with Hitler before the outbreak of World War II and thought his policies of appeasement had bought peace for the world. Instead they had but increased the appetite of an evil ruler. The report of the conference was one of peace, but it was a false peace that would not last. The temporary tranquility was just the calm before the storm. And what a storm! Jeremiah described that kind of peace, lamenting: *"They have healed also the hurt of the daughter of my people slightly, saying, Peace, peace; when there is no peace"* (Jeremiah 6:14).

Another fact that makes Israel open to the acceptance of peace negotiations is the message of peace associated with the promised Messiah. Of His rule, Isaiah wrote:

> *For unto us a child is born, unto us a son is given: and the government shall be upon his shoulder: and his name shall be called Wonderful, Counsellor, The mighty God, The everlasting Father, The Prince of Peace. Of the increase of his government and peace there shall be no end, upon the throne of David, and upon his kingdom, to order it, and to establish it with judgment and with justice from henceforth even for ever. The zeal of the LORD of hosts will perform this (Isaiah 9:6,7).*

The prophet Haggai spoke of a better day:

> *"The glory of this latter house shall be greater than of the former, saith the Lord of hosts: and in this place will I give peace, saith*

the LORD of hosts" (Hag. 2:9).

The Bible message then is one of genuine peace for the Jews in the future. For that reason, leaders of Israel who believe the prophets are conditioned to expect ultimate peace. Since they have not recognized nor accepted their true Messiah, they may be open to deception by one who seems to be able to deliver peace to the world, especially to the Middle East with security guarantees to Israel.

The Hebrew prophets warned of a false peace plan that will be accepted by the Jews near the end time. The attack upon Israel by Russia and other nations prophesied by Ezekiel for the "latter years" will come when the Jews feel secure in their land:

> *After many days thou shalt be visited: in the latter years thou shalt come into the land that is brought back from the sword, and is gathered out of many people, against the mountains of Israel, which have been always waste: but it is brought forth out of the nations, and they shall dwell safely all of them.... And thou shalt say, I will go up to the land of unwalled villages; I will go to them that are at rest, that dwell safely, all of them dwelling without walls, and having neither bars nor gates* (Ezek. 38:8,11).

Furthermore, Israel and perhaps many other nations will enter into a covenant (treaty) with the final world dictator wherein they will be guaranteed peace. The duration of the agreement will be seven years. This seven-year agreement will coincide with the seventieth week of Daniel's prophecy, and genuine peace will be short-lived. The treaty will be broken after three and one-half years, and its breaking will usher in earth's most terrible time:

> *And he shall confirm the covenant with many for one week: and in the midst of the week he shall cause the sacrifice and the oblation to cease, and for the overspreading of abominations he*

107

shall make it desolate, even until the consummation, and that determined shall be poured upon the desolate (Dan. 9:27).

Commenting on Daniel 9:27 and the efforts for peace in the Middle East, Walvoord and Walvoord have written:

"A peace settlement in the Middle East is one of the most important events predicted for the end time. The signing of this peace treaty will start the final countdown leading to Armageddon and then introduce the new world leader who will be destined to become world dictator—the infamous Antichrist. According to Daniel 9:27, the last seven years leading up to the second coming of Christ will begin with just such a peace settlement. The same passage describes a covenant to be made between the nation of Israel and the prince who will rise to power (Daniel 9:26). While the details of the covenant are not given, it will be an attempt to settle the Arab-Israeli controversy which has focused world attention on the Middle East. It may well take the form of a forced peace settlement in which Israel returns much of the land conquered through war in exchange for strong international guarantees for Israel's safety and prosperity...

The key issue in negotiations would be the city of Jerusalem itself, which Israel prizes more than any other possession. Undoubtedly there will be a strong attempt to make Jerusalem an international city with free access not only for Jews but for Christians and Muslims as well. The temple area may be internationalized, and Israel's territorial conquests will be greatly reduced. In the light of Arab power and the isolation of the United States as the sole supporting force behind Israel's continuity as a nation, it seems that any settlement short of this will not satisfy the Arab world." [1]

The ingredients then in the coming peace agreement between Israel and other Middle Eastern countries are as follows:

1. Israel will long for peace.
2. The Arabs will long for peace.
3. The world will fear the igniting of a nuclear war through a Middle East confrontation.
4. Arab wealth and power will have produced worldwide apprehension of an energy cutoff or another economy-shattering rise in the price of oil.
5. The prophets have written of a temporary peace that will come to Israel in the end time that will be broken by the Antichrist.

The peace offensive is already on. We may expect a number of lesser treaties before the tragic one involving the final world dictator. As diplomats assemble and the push for peace increases, it will be well to remember Paul's comment concerning the cry for peace at closing time: "*For when they shall say, Peace and safety; then sudden destruction cometh upon them, as travail upon a woman with child; and they shall not escape*" (1 Thessalonians 5:3).

Students of the Scriptures will remember that real peace can only come when the Prince of Peace returns. Until then there will be no lasting peace on earth. And the crescendo of peace rhetoric that has already begun is but a sign of end-time destruction, the harbinger of history's bloodiest hour—the Time of Jacob's Trouble.

11
THE TIME OF JACOB'S TROUBLE

For nearly two thousand years we have been living in a parenthesis, a prophetic interval, a time "in between."

Daniel's prophecy in the vision of the seventy weeks called for a period of 490 years when God would deal especially with Israel. When Christ offered Himself as the Prince of Israel, 483 years, or 69 weeks of years, had been fulfilled. When He was rejected and crucified the prophetic clock stopped, not to begin again until the Jews were back in their land and the parenthetical period had ended.

During this prophetic interval, sometimes known as the Church Age, both Jews and Gentiles who are born again through faith in Christ become part of the body of Christ or the bride of Christ. The signal that the "in between" time has ended will be the removal of the church (the bride of Christ) from the earth. This great event is described in a number of Bible portions. One of the clearest is 1 Thessalonians 4:13 –18:

But I would not have you to be ignorant, brethren, concerning them which are asleep, that ye sorrow not, even as others which have no hope. For if we believe that Jesus died and rose again, even so them also which sleep in Jesus will God bring with him. For this we say unto you by the word of the Lord, that we which are alive and remain unto the coming of the Lord shall not prevent them which are asleep. For the Lord himself shall descend from heaven with a shout, with the voice of the archangel, and with the trump of God: and the dead in Christ shall rise first: Then we which are alive and remain shall be caught up together with them in the clouds, to meet the Lord in the air: and so shall we ever be with the Lord. Wherefore comfort one another with these words.

The event then that ends the Church Age and ushers in the seventieth week of Daniel's prophecy is the return of Christ for His church. This coming of Christ in the air is known as the Rapture of the church; it involves the resurrection of the Christian dead as well as the exit from earth of all believers living at that time.

With the removal of the church, earth plunges into its most awful hour. Of this time Jesus said, "*For then shall be great tribulation, such as was not since the beginning of the world to this time, no, nor ever shall be*" (Matthew 24:21). He was speaking of the seven-year period known as the Tribulation, or the Time of Jacob's Trouble, so named because of Jeremiah's prophecy: "*Alas! for that day is great, so that none is like it: it is even the time of Jacob's trouble...*" (Jeremiah 30:7).

Some believe the church will remain on earth for the Tribulation. There are a number of reasons for rejecting this conclusion.

The return of Christ for His church is a sign less and always imminent event. Even the New Testament writers expected the Lord's return at any moment: "*For our conversation* [citizenship] *is in heaven; from whence also we look for the Saviour, the Lord Jesus Christ*" (Philippians 3:20).

All signs of the Lord's return have to do with the coming of Christ to set up His Kingdom. They are only indicators of the approaching Rapture because that event precedes the establishment of Christ's kingdom by seven years. The moment the Tribulation begins, however, a timetable will be evident. Date-setting will be conclusive. During the Tribulation, Christ's return will no longer be imminent. Therefore, the Rapture of the church must precede the Time of Jacob's Trouble.

The Tribulation will be a time of wrath: "*For the great day of his wrath is come; and who shall be able to stand?*" (Revelation 6:17). And the church is not to be the recipient of wrath. In assuring the Thessalonian Christians that they would not go through the Tribulation, Paul explained: "*For God hath not appointed us to wrath, but to obtain salvation by our Lord Jesus Christ*" (1 Thessalonians. 5:9).

Wicked as it is, the world is not quite ready for the Tribulation and the Antichrist. The church is not all it ought to be, but the world is better because the church is here. Sin is rampant, but it would be far worse without the presence of the church and its hindering influence to evil: "*For the mystery of iniquity doth already work: only he who now letteth will let* [hinder], *until he be taken out of the way. And then shall that Wicked be revealed...*" (2 Thessalonians 2:7,8).

The Holy Spirit, working through Christians, holds back the tide of evil sweeping the world. When His influence in this manner is removed at the Rapture, the world will be ready for the Antichrist and the Tribulation.

The church has three heavenly appointments during the earthly Tribulation.

First, Christians cannot be on earth during the Tribulation because they have important business elsewhere. When the Lord returns for His church, it will be time for the judgment seat of Christ: "*And behold, I come quickly; and my reward is with me, to give every man according as his work shall be*" (Revelation 22:12).

Second, Christians who are living at the time of Christ's return must have time in the mansions prepared by Jesus as described in John 14:1-3. The only time available for the fulfillment of this promise before the Millennium is during the Tribulation.

Third, the marriage supper of the Lamb will take place in heaven during the end of the Tribulation period, according to Revelation 19:9, and the bride of Christ must attend. Following this joyful occasion, those who belong to Christ will return with Him as He comes to set up His kingdom. Since believers must come from heaven to earth at the end of the Tribulation, it is clear that the Rapture must precede that time of trouble.

Finally, it must be remembered that the Tribulation is especially related to Israel. Once this truth is established, all confusion about the time of the Rapture disappears. The return of Christ for His church marks the end of the Church Age, the parenthetical period, and begins the Time of Jacob's Trouble.

What is the Time of Jacob's Trouble? Let Daniel describe it: "...*there shall be a time of trouble, such as never was since there was a nation even to that same time...*" (Daniel 12:1).

This unprecedented period of tribulation is not to be confused with daily tribulations which all of God's people pass through. Jesus said: "...*In the world ye shall have tribulation: but be of good cheer; I have overcome the world*" (John 16:33).

Paul had learned to glory in tribulations: "...*we glory in tribulations also: knowing that tribulation worketh patience*" (Romans 5:3).

These heartaches, problems, and tribulations are different from the Tribulation. This seven-year period is one of immense suffering for the entire world. It is an era of unthinkable trouble. Nothing in history can be compared to it, nor will there ever be anything equal to it in the future. Chapters 6, 8, 9, 15, and 16 of Revelation describe the Time of Jacob's Trouble under the headings of seven seals, seven trumpets, and seven vials. Next week we will look at the panorama of human pain that will be experienced by the inhabitants of the earth during the Tribulation.

First Seal

And I saw when the Lamb opened one of the seals.... and behold a white horse: and he that sat on him had a bow; and a crown was given unto him: and he went forth conquering, and to conquer (Rev.6:1,2).

113

Second Seal

And when he had opened the second seal.... there went out another horse that was red: and power was given to him that sat thereon to take peace from the earth, and that they should kill one another (Rev. 6:3,4)

Third Seal

And when he had opened the third seal.... lo a black horse; and he that sat on him had a pair of balances in his hand. And I heard a voice in the midst of the four beasts say, A measure of wheat for a penny, and three measures of barley for a penny; and see thou hurt not the oil and the wine (Rev. 6:5,6).

Fourth Seal

And when he had opened the fourth seal.... behold a pale horse: and his name that sat on him was Death, and Hell followed with him. And power was given unto them over the fourth part of the earth, to kill with sword, and with hunger, and with death, and with the beasts of the earth (Rev. 6:7,8).

Fifth Seal

And when he had opened the fifth seal, I saw under the altar the souls of them that were slain for the word of God, and for the testimony which they held: And they cried with a loud voice, saying, How long, O Lord, holy and true, dost thou not judge and avenge our blood on them that dwell on the earth? (Rev. 6:9,10)

Sixth Seal

And I beheld when he had opened the sixth seal, and, lo, there was a great earthquake; and the sun became black as sackcloth of hair, and the moon became as blood; And the stars of heaven fell unto the earth, even as a fig tree casteth her untimely figs,

114

when she is shaken of a mighty wind. And the heaven departed as a scroll when it is rolled together; and every mountain and island were moved out of their places. And the kings of the earth, and the great men, and the rich men, and the chief captains, and the mighty men, and every bondman, and every free man, hid themselves in the dens and in the rocks of the mountains; And said to the mountains and rocks, Fall on us, and hide us from the face of him that sitteth on the throne, and from the wrath of the Lamb: For the great day of his wrath is come; and who shall be able to stand? (Rev. 6:12-17)

Seventh Seal

The seventh seal, described in Revelation 8:1, depicts the lull before the storm. The catastrophic trumpet judgments are so horrendous that all heaven sits in awesome silence before the blitzkrieg begins. That is why the text reports, *"there was silence in heaven about the space of half an hour."* Then each of the seven angels sounds a trumpet before each calamitous judgment begins.

First Trumpet

The first angel sounded, and there followed hail and fire mingled with blood, and they were cast upon the earth: and the third part of trees was burnt up, and all green grass was burnt up (Rev. 8:7).

Second Trumpet

And the second angel sounded, and as it were a great mountain burning with fire was cast into the sea: and the third part of the sea became blood; And the third part of the creatures which were in the sea, and had life, died; and the third part of the ships were destroyed (Rev. 8:8,9).

Third Trumpet

And the third angel sounded, and there fell a great star from heaven, burning as it were a lamp, and it fell upon the third part of the rivers, and upon the fountains of waters; And the name of the star is called Wormwood: and the third part of the waters became wormwood; and many men died of the waters, because they were made bitter (Rev. 8:10,11).

Fourth Trumpet

And the fourth angel sounded, and the third part of the sun was smitten, and the third part of the moon, and the third part of the stars; so as the third part of them was darkened, and the day shone not for a third part of it, and the night likewise. And I beheld, and heard an angel flying through the midst of heaven, saying with a loud voice, Woe, woe, woe, to the inhabiters of the earth by reason of the other voices of the trumpet of the three angels, which are yet to sound! (Rev. 8:12,13).

Fifth Trumpet

And the fifth angel sounded, and I saw a star fall from heaven unto the earth: and to him was given the key of the bottomless pit. And he opened the bottomless pit; and there arose a smoke out of the pit, as the smoke of a great furnace; and the sun and the air were darkened by reason of the smoke of the pit. And there came out of the smoke locusts upon the earth: and unto them was given power, as the scorpions of the earth have power. And it was commanded them that they should not hurt the grass of the earth, neither any green thing, neither any tree; but only those men which have not the seal of God in their foreheads. And to them it was given that they should not kill them, but that they should be tormented five months: and their torment was as the torment of a scorpion, when he striketh a man. And in those days shall men seek death, and shall not

116

find it; and shall desire to die, and death shall flee from them (Rev. 9:1-6).

Sixth Trumpet

And the sixth angel sounded, and I heard a voice from the four horns of the golden altar which is before God, Saying to the sixth angel which had the trumpet, Loose the four angels which are bound in the great river Euphrates. And the four angels were loosed, which were prepared for an hour, and a day, and a month, and a year, for to slay the third part of men. And the number of the army of the horsemen were two hundred thousand thousand: and I heard the number of them. And thus I saw the horses in the vision, and them that sat on them, having breastplates of fire, and of jacinth, and brimstone: and the heads of the horses were as the heads of lions; and out of their mouths issued fire and smoke and brimstone. By these three was the third part of men killed, by the fire, and by the smoke, and by the brimstone, which issued out of their mouths. For their power is in their mouth, and in their tails: for their tails were like unto serpents, and had heads, and with them they do hurt (Rev. 9:13-19).

Seventh Trumpet

And the seventh angel sounded; and there were great voices in heaven, saying, The kingdoms of this world are become the kingdoms of our Lord, and of his Christ; and he shall reign for ever and ever.... And the temple of God was opened in heaven, and there was seen in his temple the ark of his testament: and there were lightnings, and voices, and thunderings, and an earthquake, and great hail (Rev. 11:15,19).

The blast of the seventh trumpet also begins the seven vial judgments. They are as follows:

First Vial

And the first went, and poured out his vial upon the earth; and there fell a noisome and grievous sore upon the men which had the mark of the beast, and upon them which worshipped his image (Rev. 16:2).

Second Vial

And the second angel poured out his vial upon the sea; and it became as the blood of a dead man: and every living soul died in the sea (Rev. 16:3).

Third Vial

And the third angel poured out his vial upon the rivers and fountains of waters; and they became blood (Rev. 16:4).

Fourth Vial

And the fourth angel poured out his vial upon the sun; and power was given unto him to scorch men with fire. And men were scorched with great heat, and blasphemed the name of God, which hath power over these plagues: and they repented not to give him glory (Rev. 16:8,9).

Fifth Vial

And the fifth angel poured out his vial upon the seat of the beast; and his kingdom was full of darkness; and they gnawed their tongues for pain, And blasphemed the God of heaven because of their pains and their sores, and repented not of their deeds (Rev. 16:10,11).

Sixth Vial

And the sixth angel poured out his vial upon the great river

Euphrates; and the water thereof was dried up, that the way of the kings of the east might be prepared (Rev. 16:12).

Seventh Vial

And the seventh angel poured out his vial into the air; and there came a great voice out of the temple of heaven, from the throne, saying, It is done. And there were voices, and thunders, and lightnings; and there was a great earthquake, such as was not since men were upon the earth, so mighty an earthquake, and so great. And the great city was divided into three parts, and the cities of the nations fell: and great Babylon came in remembrance before God, to give unto her the cup of the wine of the fierceness of his wrath. And every island fled away, and the mountains were not found. And there fell upon men a great hail out of heaven, every stone about the weight of a talent: and men blasphemed God because of the plague of the hail; for the plague thereof was exceeding great (Rev. 16:17-21).

Seals, trumpets, and vials, what do they mean?

The seals speak of the political, economic, and religious problems that will occur during the Tribulation. A world leader appears who seems to have the answers for peace. He rides a white horse.

Commenting on the first seal, Dr. H. A. Ironside wrote:

"This rider on the white horse evidently pictures man's last effort to bring in a reign of order and peace while Christ is still rejected. It will be the world's greatest attempt to pull things together after the church is gone. It will be the Devil's cunning scheme for bringing in a mock millennium without Christ." [1]

The second seal reveals that this peace is short-lived. One who rides a red horse is given power to take peace from the earth and a terrible war follows.

The third seal announces famine, inflation, and shortages, well-known companions of war.

The fourth seal announces plagues, sicknesses, and all kinds of violence, bringing death to many.

The fifth seal reveals religious persecution and indicates that multitudes will be martyred during this terrible time.

The sixth seal pictures ecological upheavals that challenge description. Generations of pollution combined with the problems in nature brought on by nuclear warfare may contribute to the chaos in nature pictured here. However, it is clear that the wrath of God is the moving force in this frightening rebellion of the creation *"For the great day of his wrath is to come; and who shall be able to stand?"*(Revelation 6:17).

The trumpets sound the coming of divine judgments. The Tribulation period is a time of wrath—God's wrath. And the plagues that descend are reminiscent of those brought upon Pharaoh by the hand of Moses under the direction of God. There is hail and fire mingled with blood. Trees and grass are burned. Water is turned to blood. Great turbulence comes to the sea, destroying ships and marine life. There are disturbances in the heavens and on earth. The stars fall. Darkness descends. Demonic activity is widespread. An army of unprecedented size, numbering 200 million, moves from the east toward Jerusalem. It will be a fearsome time to be alive.

The vials constitute an outpouring of God's wrath upon the earth toward the end of the Tribulation period, and the results are mind-boggling.

People who have received the mark of the Beast, the Antichrist, are afflicted with painful sores that are evidently incurable. Perhaps this is a universal reaction to receiving the mysterious mark of the Beast in the hand or the forehead—some allergic affliction that falls upon all who have been imprinted with this satanic skin-credit-card that allows them to buy and sell during the Time of Jacob's Trouble.

The sea, once the source of food for man and his supposed hope for the future as a reservoir of nutrients, becomes as the blood of a dead man and every living thing in the sea dies.

The rivers and springs of the earth turn to blood as a judgment against the wicked Tribulation regime that has shed the blood of righteous people.

The sun, which has befriended earth's citizens through the centuries, becomes their enemy, scorching men.

Intense darkness comes upon the earth, accompanied by unbearable pain, causing ungodly people to blaspheme God. The Euphrates River is dried up and a huge army from the east marches through the dry riverbed on its way to Jerusalem.

Electrical storms and earthquakes that dwarf all such manifestations of nature in the past strike the earth with ferocity, destroying cities and causing nations to fall.

The wrath of God is revealed from heaven against the Antichrist and his kingdom.

The Beast

The rise of the Antichrist, the Beast, is the most significant cant political event during the Time of Jacob's Trouble. He is described by John in Revelation 13 as the beast that rises out of the sea, having seven heads and ten horns. The prophets call for him to emerge from the revived Roman Empire. And Daniel spoke of him as the "little horn" whose power would reach its zenith for three and one-half years.

Having guaranteed peace to Israel, temporarily settling the Middle East problem and putting down all rebellion, the Beast gains the allegiance of the entire world. His domination of the oil-rich Middle East will allow him to control the economies of the world, reaching even to the simple routines of life such as buying and selling food or clothing. A special mark in the hand or forehead will be required for all to transact any business.

> *And he causeth all, both small and great, rich and poor, free and bond, to receive a mark in their right hand, or in their foreheads: And that no man might buy or sell, save he that had the mark, or the name of the beast, or the number of his name. Here is wisdom. Let him that hath understanding count the number of the beast: for it is the number of a man; and his number is Six hundred threescore and six* (Rev. 13:16-18).

The false religious system that prospers during the early part of the reign of the Antichrist is described in Revelation 17. This blasphemous ecclesiastical empire will thrive on pomp and ceremony and will give allegiance to the irreverent final world dictator, the Beast.

But the work of God does not cease during the Time of Jacob's Trouble. Shortly after the Rapture there will be a remnant of Jews who turn to Christ. The initial number is 144,000—12,000 from each of the tribes of Israel. These converted Jews are called "servants of God" and they are extremely successful in ministering to others. Not long after this elect group is announced by John, he describes a great multitude from all nations who have been converted to Christ as a result of their labor and who are willing to prove their faith through martyrdom.

It is interesting that many Jews who do not turn to Christ during the Tribulation will return to temple worship as in Old Testament times, including the sacrifice of animals. It may be that allowing the erection of this temple in Jerusalem will be a part of the peace agreement between the final world dictator and the Jews.

Ultimately, however, the Antichrist will destroy the false church and will take control of Jewish worship, declaring himself to be God and demanding worship from the Jews in their own temple. The prophet Daniel spoke of this act of blasphemy as the "*abomination of desolation*" (Dan. 12:11). And Jesus warned that this would mean untold suffering for the Jews:

> *When ye therefore shall see the abomination of desolation, spoken of by Daniel the prophet, stand in the holy place, (whoso readeth, let him understand:) Then let them which be in Judea flee into the mountains: Let him which is on the housetop not come down to take any thing out of his house: Neither let him which is in the field return back to take his clothes. And woe unto them that are with child, and to them that give suck in those days! But pray ye that your flight be not in the winter, neither on the sabbath day: For then shall be great tribulation, such as was not since the beginning of the world to this time, no, nor ever shall be. And except those days shall be shortened, there should no flesh be saved: but for the elect's sake those days shall be shortened* (Matthew 24:15-22).

The peacemaker then, the Antichrist, will break his covenant or treaty with the Jews and will become their enemy and persecutor. Anti-Semitism will flourish, and Israel will experience her final holocaust.

But what event gives the Antichrist reason to break his pact of peace?

Who tampers with the tranquility established in Israel and the Middle East by this powerful end-time ruler?

What nation introduces war to the Time of Jacob's Trouble?

12
THE COMING WAR WITH RUSSIA

Russia will invade Israel at a time when war is not expected.

Students of Bible prophecy have long expected a Russian military move in the Middle East. Early in the 20th century, Dr. Ironside wrote:

> "In the last days, the final head of the Russian people will look with covetous eyes upon the great developments in the land of Palestine. They will determine that Russia must have her part of the wealth there produced. Consequently, we have the picture of a vast army, augmented by warriors from Persia, Cush, Phut, marching down toward Palestine." [1]

Aggressors in Conflict

But why have prophetic experts come to this conclusion?

The reasons are found in chapters 38 and 39 of Ezekiel's prophecy. There a devastating war is described that takes place in the Middle East involving Israel, Russia, and a number of other nations. The following is Ezekiel's indictment of the aggressors in the conflict:

> *And the word of the LORD came unto me, saying, Son of man, set thy face against Gog, the land of Magog, the chief prince of Meshech and Tubal, and prophesy against him, And say, Thus saith the Lord God; Behold, I am against thee, O Gog, the chief prince of Meshech and Tubal: And I will turn thee back, and*

put hooks into thy jaws, and I will bring thee forth, and all thine
army, horses and horsemen, all of them clothed with all sorts of
amour, even a great company with bucklers and shields, all of
them handling swords: Persia, Ethiopia, and Libya with them;
all of them with shield and helmet: Gomer, and all his bands:
and many people with thee... (Ezekiel 38:1-6)

It is no secret that the majority of prophetic speakers and writers identify the prime mover among these nations named by Ezekiel as Russia. Millions of booklets, pamphlets, and books have been circulated describing the coming war between Russia and Israel. But is there hard evidence that the conclusions of these students of prophecy are correct?

Did Ezekiel really foresee Russia rising as a military power in the end time and having a special interest in the Middle East, or have present-day writers and speakers simply used today's international tensions as an opportunity to sell books and attract crowds?

Is the public the victim of ecclesiastical opportunists who have themselves set the stage for what they describe as the end-time drama?

How can anyone be sure that Ezekiel's prophecy has anything to do with modern nations when the words used in his description of this conflict are so unfamiliar to today's Bible reader?

Who is Gog? Where is the land of Magog? Where would one look on a map to find the cities of Meshech and Tubal? To what nations did Ezekiel refer when he wrote of Gomer and Togarmah?

Unless these questions can be answered satisfactorily, there is good reason to question the conclusions being so widely accepted and promoted in our time.

Convincing Evidence

Let us begin at the beginning. A table of nations is given in

Genesis 10. At the opening of this important chapter, we are confronted with the key names in Ezekiel's prophecy: "*Now these are the generations of the sons of Noah, Shem, Ham, and Japheth: and unto them were sons born after the flood. The sons of Japheth; Gomer, and Magog, and Madai, and Javan, and Tubal, and Meshech, and Tiras*" (Genesis 10:1, 2).

These key verses describe the repopulating of the earth after the flood. It was the custom in ancient times for the descendents of a man to adopt his name for their tribe. Understanding this, historians and Bible students have been able to trace the movements of some of the tribes and know where their descendents can be found today. Using this system, the editors of the *Scofield Reference Bible* have furnished the following information about the names that concern us in the table of nations:

> Magog—"From Magog are descended the ancient Scythians or Tarters, whose descendents predominate in modern Russia."
>
> Tubal—"Tubal's descendents peopled the region south of the Black Sea from whence they spread north and south. It is probable that Tobolsk perpetuates the tribal name."
>
> Meshech—"Progenitor of a race mentioned in connection with Tubal, Magog, and other northern nations. Broadly speaking, Russia, excluding the conquests of Peter the Great and his successors, is the modern land of Magog, Tubal, and Meshech." [2]

The *Scofield Reference Bible* was published in 1909. These notes alone let us know that the identification of Russia as the main aggressor in Ezekiel's end-time battle is not the conclusion of prophetic opportunists. But there is more.

In the orient al tongue, the name of the Caucasus Mountains that run through Russia means "Fort of Gog" or "Gog's last stand." If you were to ask a Russian what he calls the heights of the Caucasus Mountains, he would say, "the Gogh."

The evidence builds.

The word that is translated "chief' in Ezekiel 38:3 is "Rosh" in the Hebrew language. For centuries prophetic scholars have generally agreed that the word "Rosh" is a proper name. Allowing this long-accepted conclusion in the translation of this verse would make it read, *"And say, Thus saith the Lord God; Behold, I am against thee, O Gog, the Rosh prince of Meshech and Tubal."*

But who is Rosh?

"Rosh" was the name of the tribe dwelling in the area of the Volga. And "Rosh" is the word for "Russia" today in some languages of the world. In Belgium and Holland it is "Rus." Here, abbreviated, it's "Russ," and often appears in that form in the headlines of newspapers. An understanding of this truth moved Robert Lowth, Bishop of London two hundred years ago, to write: "Rosh, taken as a proper name in Ezekiel signifies the inhabitants of Scythia from whom the modern Russians derive their modern name. The name 'Russia' dates only fro m the seventeenth century and was formed from the ancient name 'Russ.' [3]

It is clear then that Ezekiel was delivering a warning to the Russian prince (leader) of Meshech and Tubal.

We have already seen from Scofield's notes of 1909 that Tubal is the root of the name Tobolsk, but what about Meshech? In his note on Ezekiel 38:2, Scofield continues his work of identification, stating: "That the primary reference is to the northern European powers headed by Russia, all agree... Gog is the prince, Magog his land, the reference to Meshech and Tubal (Moscow and Tobolsk) is a clear mark of identification." [4]

As has been already shown, Dr. Scofield was by no means the first to come to this conclusion. In 1890, Arno C. Gaebelein wrote a book on Ezekiel. Commenting on chapters 38 and 39, he declared: "This is Russia, Moscow, and Tobolsk."

Another important voice of the past is that of Josephus. In Book I, Chapter VI of his work, this historian who lived almost two thousand years ago stated that the Scythians were called Magogites by the Greeks. Why is that important? The Scythians populated Russia.

It is little wonder then that the weight of prophetic scholarship has gone with the conclusion that Russia is the chief aggressor named by Ezekiel in this end-time war with Israel. The allies of Russia in that fierce conflict will be Persia (Iran and Iraq), Ethiopia, Libya, Gomer (Eastern Germany and Slovakia), and Togarmah (Turkey).

It is interesting that Daniel adds Egypt to the names of nations coming against Israel and the final world dictator, so that the invasion includes attacks from the north and the south, as well as the prospect of trouble from the east (see Dan. 11:40-44).

There is no need to marshal the scholars of the past to confirm the place or purpose of this war. Ezekiel explained:

> *After many days thou shalt be visited: in the latter years thou shalt come into the land that is brought back from the sword, and is gathered out of many people, against the mountains of Israel, which have been always waste: but it is broug ht forth out of the nations, and they shall dwell safely all of them* (Ezek. 38:8).

What a clear and up-to-date description of Israel! She is certainly the land that is brought back from the sword—gathered out of many people—a former wasteland—brought forth out of the nations.

The invaders of Israel will come with immense air power: "Thou shalt ascend and come like a storm, thou shalt be like a cloud to cover the land, thou, and all thy bands, and many people with thee" (Ezek. 38:9).

They will also come in full confidence of victory:

> *And thou shalt say, I will go up to the land of unwalled vil-*

lages; I will go to them that are at rest, that dwell safely, all of them dwelling without walls, and having neither bars nor gates, To take a spoil, and to take a prey; to turn thine hand upon the desolate places that are now inhabited, and upon the people that are gathered out of the nations, which have gotten cattle and goods, that dwell in the midst of the land (Ezek. 38:11,12).

The Unfolding Mystery

The purpose of this war has long caused questions for commentators. Ezekiel explains the purpose to be twofold: to take a spoil and to take a prey. The poverty of Palestine has made this difficult to understand, but now the mystery is unfolding.

The Jews have been the prey of persecutors for thousands of years. Today, if it were militarily possible, they would be the prey of their Arab neighbors. In the coming war with Russia, nearly all the Arab nations will be allies of Russia, and their primary purpose will be to take a prey—Israel. The Russians, however, will be marching to the Middle East to take a spoil. They will be pleased to cooperate in the conquest of Israel, knowing that when their military forces overrun the Middle East they will control all the wealth there, including the Arab oil.

Recent history has demonstrated that those who become the allies of Russia are soon totally controlled by her; witness Eastern Europe. So while the Arabs will join the attack against Israel to take a prey, Russia will be invading to take a spoil.

And the spoil is oil.

In addition, the mineral wealth of the Dead Sea, valued at two trillion dollars, must be considere d, as well as the wealth being generated in Israel through industry and agriculture. The protest of Israel's allies makes this clear:

Sheba, and Dedan, and the merchants of Tarshish, with all the

young lions thereof, shall say unto thee, Art thou come to take a
spoil? hast thou gathered thy company to take a prey? to carry
away silver and gold, and take away cattle and goods, to take
a great spoil? (Ezek. 38:13)

Sheba and Dedan represent a small number of Arabs who will not participate in the attack on Israel. The merchants of Tarshish are Western powers who by this time will be under the control of the Antichrist, soon to be revealed for who he is and to become the final world dictator.

Important Timing

When will this war take place?

There are four time factors that allow us to arrive at the approximate time of the war between Russia and Israel.

1. The war takes place in the "latter years" (38:8), or the "latter days" (38:16).
2. The war can only take place when the Jews are in their land. This prophecy could not have been fulfilled before 1948. Any invasion of the Middle East by Russia previous to statehood for Israel would have been meaningless in regard to this prophecy. The enactment of this scene in the last days also guarantees the survival of Israel until the war with Russia. Were the Arabs to succeed in destroying the Jews, it would be impossible to fulfill Ezekiel's prophecy.
3. At the time of the invasion of Israel, Russia must be a major military power, a fact that guarantees the survival of Russia until the war with Israel. The increase of Russian military might is well known, but that immense and fearsome buildup would have no prophetic significance if the Jews were not in their homeland. Conversely, the gigantic Russian arms effort in view of the present

Middle East situation must be seen as preliminary to an attack on Israel as prophesied by Ezekiel.

4. This war between Russia and Israel must take place when the Jews are dwelling securely in their land. The threat of Arab invasion will therefore have been removed to the point that the Jews feel safe: "*And thou shalt say, I will go up to the land of unwalled villages; I will go to them that are at rest, that dwell safely, all of them dwelling without walls, and having neither bars nor gates*" (Ezek. 38:11).

It seems likely that this Jewish security will come from enacting a treaty with the head of the Western alliance or the revived Roman Empire. It will be an agreement intended to last for seven years: "*...And he shall confirm the covenant with many for one week...* " (Dan. 9:27).

Since by the time of the Russian attack, the treaty of peace will have been in force long enough for the Jews to feel safe, it appears that the Russian invasion will come at about the middle of the Tribulation period or approximately three and one-half years after its signing. There is also a hint that the Antichrist will come to world power at that point in time. The extension of his dominion over all the earth seems to follow the defeat of Russia and the armies of the East (Rev. 9:16).

Russia's attack on Israel will be her greatest military blunder. Though brief, the conflict will be one of the most destructive in history. Ezekiel's description of the battle is as follows:

...Surely in that day there shall be a great shaking in the land of Israel; So that the fishes of the sea, and the fowls of the heaven, and the beasts of the field, and all creeping things that creep upon the earth, and all the men that are upon the face of the earth, shall shake at my presence, and the mountains shall be thrown down, and the steep places shall fall, and every wall

131

shall fall to the ground. And I will call for a sword against him through all my mountains, saith the Lord God: every man's sword shall be against his brother. And I will plead against him with pestilence and with blood; and I will rain upon him, and upon his bands, and upon the many people that are with him, an overflowing rain, and great hailstones, fire, and brimstone (Ezek. 38:19-22).

The prophet's vision carries with it many of the characteristics of nuclear war. There are earth-splitting explosions. Mountains are toppled. Rain, hail, and fire become part of the picture as nature erupts in rebellion against the forces marching to bring destruction to the Jews.

While details of military action in this war are few, something about the defeat of the northern invaders will make it clear to the Jews that God has protected them: *"Thus will I magnify myself, and sanctify myself; and I will be known in the eyes of many nations, and they shall know that I am the LORD* (Ezek. 38:23).

The casualties of the Russian invaders are so great that only one-sixth of the fighting force is left after the battle: *"And I will turn thee back, and l eave but the sixth part of thee, and will cause thee to come up from the north parts, and will bring thee upon the mountains of Israel"* (Ezek. 39:2).

Two important developments will follow the defeat of the invaders of Israel. First, the attack by Russia will give the Antichrist an excuse for full occupation of Israel under the pretense of protection and will, along with his defeat of the huge Eastern force (Rev. 9:16), extend his power over the entire world. Second, the divine protection of Israel as prophesied by Ezekiel and proclaimed to the world by evangelists and writers throughout the closing time will turn many Jews to their Messiah, the Lord Jesus Christ.

The remaining forty-two months of the Tribulation will show man at his worst.

The final world dictator will become the most evil of all

earth's political and religious leaders. His blasphemy, oppression, and self-exaltation will surpass that of all tyrants before him.

Persecution of believers in Christ will reach an all-time high. Millions will be martyred.

Anti-Semitism will become the passion of those in power.

And the world will continue its age-old march to the most fierce and foolish war of all—the Battle of Armageddon.

13
ARMAGEDDON

"Armageddon" has come to stand for the most terrible of all wars. The word actually means "mount of Megiddo," referring to a small mountain overlooking the Mediterranean Sea. The great valley there has been been a battlefield for many conquerors and it will be the focal point of the earth's final conflict.

Since the fall of man, earth's population has been training for Armageddon. Every tiny skirmish and world war has been a preliminary to the battle of battles: Armageddon.

Following the defeat of Russia and her armies by Israel, the final world dictator, the Antichrist, will be revealed for who he is—a ruthless, satanically controlled, evil person. The length of his reign after the Israeli defeat of Russia will be three and one-half years (forty-two months; see Rev. 13:5) and during that time he will bring the world to its most violent hour.

The World's Most Violent Hour

There is considerable speculation as to just what triggers the Battle of Armageddon. Why do the armies of the world gather in the Middle East at the end of the Tribulation period? Is there a rebellion in the kingdom of the Antichrist? What precipitates the final conflict? Although there is mystery tery surrounding some of these questions, there are a number of certainties about Armageddon.

1. It takes place at the end of the Tribulation (Rev. 16:16).
2. It involves all the nations of the world (Joel 3:12).
3. It pits all nations against the Lord and His anointed (Ps. 2).
4. It ends with the revelation of Christ as King of Kings and Lord of Lords (Rev. 19:11-21).

While many events of the end time are hidden from us, it is not difficult to sort out some important developments during the Tribulation period that lead to the Battle of Armageddon.

1. The Consolidation of the Power of the Antichrist

When the Beast (the Antichrist) makes peace with Israel and guarantees her security at the beginning of Daniel's seventieth week, he is not in complete control of the world. Although he is headed for ultimate dictatorship, the earth is at that time still given to considerable nationalism. The Beast will have to fight for total control of the earth. To gain unchallenged dominion, he will have to face the military might of both the Russian confederacy and a powerful Eastern force, probably China. Writing of this international turmoil, Daniel explained: *"And at the time of the end shall the king of the south push at him: and the king of the north shall come against him like a whirlwind, with chariots, and with horsemen, and with many ships; and he shall enter into the countries, and shall overflow and pass over"* (Dan. 11:40).

That this crisis is not confined to the northern alliance is made clear by Daniel 11:44: *"But tidings out of the east and out of the north shall trouble him: therefore he shall go forth with great fury to destroy, and utterly to make away many."*

Following the miraculous defeat of the Russian armies and their allies for Israel's sake, the Antichrist will vent his fury against the massive Eastern force of 200 million that is moving toward the Middle East to challenge his power. The casualties in this confrontation will total one-third of the world's population. Here is John's description of the struggle and slaughter:

> "And the four angels were loosed, which were prepared for an hour, and a day, and a month, and a year, for to slay the third part of men. And the number of the army of the horsemen were two hundred thousand thousand: and I heard the number of them. And thus I saw the horses in the vision, and them that sat on them, having breastplates of fire, and of jacinth, and brimstone: and the heads of the horses were as the heads of lions; and out of their mouths issued fire and smoke and brimstone. By these three was the third part of men killed, by the fire, and by the smoke, and by the brimstone, which issued out of their mouths. For this power is in their mouth, and in their tails: for their tails were like unto serpents, and had heads, and with them they do hurt" (Rev. 9:15-19).

It is not difficult to envision nuclear weaponry here, and in the populous Eastern nations the destruction unleashed by the Antichrist will be dreadful.

With all the world subservient to him, the final world dictator will deify himself, demanding worship in the Jews' temple in Jerusalem. He will then assume total economic control, requiring his mark in the hand or forehead in order for a person to transact any business. The Beast will rule the earth, assisted by the false prophet and energized by Satan. The entire world will be under the control of a satanic trinity:

> "And they worshipped the dragon which gave power unto the beast: and they worshipped the beast, saying, Who is like unto the beast? who is able to make war with him? And there was given unto him a mouth speaking great things and blasphemies; and power was given unto him to continue forty and two months. And he opened his mouth in blasphemy against

God, to blaspheme his name, and his tabernacle, and them that dwell in heaven. And it was given unto him to make war with the saints, and to overcome them: and power was given him over all kindreds, and tongues, and nations. And all that dwell upon the earth shall worship him, whose names are not written in the book of life of the Lamb slain from the foundation of the world" (Rev. 13:4-8).

It is clear then that all opposition to the Beast will finally be put down, making him a world dictator. Threats from the north, the south, and the east will be overcome. "...*therefore he shall go forth with great fury to destroy, and utterly to make away many. And he shall plant the tabernacles of his palace between the seas in the glorious mountain...*" (Dan. 11:44,45).

The Antichrist will have accomplished the dream of Hitler, Napoleon, the Caesars, and others. He will be dictator of the world.

2. The 144,000 Converted Jews

Another important factor as the world moves toward Armageddon will be the conversion to Christ of 144,000 Jews—12,000 from each of the twelve tribes of Israel (see Rev. 7). The result of their missionary activity during history's most difficult time will be phenomenal. They will reap converts from all nations, even though conversion will mean martyrdom for many (Rev. 7:9-17).

The message of these 144,000 Hebrew Christian evangelists will be the gospel of the kingdom—that is, it will be the gospel with a kingdom emphasis. They will be announcing the coming kingdom of Christ, and during their ministry Matthew 24:14 will be fulfilled: "And this gospel of the kingdom shall be preached in all the world for a witness unto all nations; and then shall the end come."

In his book, *The Jews and Armageddon*, Milton B. Lindberg

137

describes the work of the 144,000 Jews as follows:

> "The Gospel of Christ has a number of descriptive designations because of a variety of emphases. In Matthew 24 it is called the "gospel of the kingdom" because the emphasis in its proclamation will be upon the Saviour's near return to set up His kingdom.... How these redeemed sons of Israel will delight to proclaim the good news of salvation with the added emphasis that at last the long-looked-for kingdom is about to be established. At long last, the Messianic hopes of Israel are to be realized. Jerusalem is to be the capital of Messiah's kingdom. Israel's Messiah is to be king over all the earth (Zech. 14:9)." [1]

An added dimension to the kingdom message of the 144,000 servants of God will be their ability to announce the approximate time of the Lord's return. Tribulation chronology will make this possible.

A number of prophecies state that the rule of the final world dictator will continue for three and one-half years after breaking the agreement for peace with Israel. Daniel described this period as "*a time and times and the dividing of time*" (Dan. 7:25). John similarly spoke of "a time, and times, and a half a time" (Rev. 12:14). Becoming more specific, he wrote: "*And there was given unto him a mouth speaking great things and blasphemies; and power was given unto him to continue forty and two months*" (Rev. 13:5).

Armed then with the evidence of fulfilled prophecy and the unfolding Tribulation drama, these end-time messengers will reap a great harvest. To quote Lindberg again:

> "When the 144,000 begin to preach the Gospel, they will be given a hearing. Even today the world loves to hear the testimony of those who, like Paul, having hated Christ and persecuted the church, now proclaim the grace of God.

Not only will these transformed Jews have a hearing, but as Revelation 7 indicates, their preaching will result in "a great multitude, which no man could number, of all nations, and kindreds, and people, and tongues" coming out of the Great Tribulation, having "washed their robes, and made them white in the blood of the Lamb." What a mighty revival will result when these enemies of Jesus Christ become His devoted servants! Onward sweeps the revival in mighty power, drawing multitudes to faith in Christ." [2]

It is not difficult to imagine the reaction of the world dictator to these who publicly proclaim the end of his reign and announce the coming kingdom of Christ. His anger will explode in an avalanche of persecution. Multitudes will be martyred. There will be no Sunday-go-to-meeting Christians during the Tribulation. Great numbers will be called upon to seal their testimonies with blood.

3. The Impact of the Defeat of Russia

The deliverance of the Jews from the Russian invaders will cause many of them to turn to Christ, claiming Him as their Messiah and Lord: *"So the house of Israel shall know that I am the LORD their God from that day and forward"* (Ezekiel 39:22).

This desertion of the dictator by numbers of Jews will intensify his hatred of both Jews and Christians, especially Jews who have been converted to Christ. A wave of anti-Semitism will sweep the earth, motivated by Satan and promoted by the Antichrist: *"And the dragon was wroth with the woman [Israel], and went to make war with the remnant of her seed, which keep the commandments of God, and have the testimony of Jesus Christ"* (Revelation 12:17).

4. The Two Witnesses

The Antichrist and his kingdom will bring great trouble to the earth. But he will also be troubled. Irritations will increase with the message of Christ's imminent return preached throughout the world. Every tribe and nation will be made aware of the time-table of the end, the eventual fall of the Antichrist, and the coming kingdom of Christ. To add to his miseries, two powerful prophets will appear in Jerusalem and will witness there for three and one-half years, guaranteeing the truth of the kingdom message of the 144,000 servants of God.

The identity of the two witnesses has caused great specu-lation, with general agreement that one of them will be Elijah: *"Behold, I will send you Elijah the prophet before the coming of the great and dreadful day of the Lord"* (Malachi 4:5).

The other witness is usually thought to be either Enoch or Moses.

Those who choose Enoch do so because like Elijah he did not die (Hebrews 11:5), and it is thought that his exemption from death was in view of his coming martyrdom during the great Tribulation. His message must also be considered. Evidently this prophet had been given a revelation of the second coming of Christ and had announced it to his generation:

> *"And Enoch also, the seventh from Adam, prophesied of these, saying, Behold, the Lord cometh with ten thousands of his saints, To execute judgment upon all, and to convince all that are ungodly among them of all their ungodly deeds which they have ungodly committed, and of all their hard speeches which ungodly sinners have spoken against him"* (Jude 14,15).

Some build a strong case for Moses, citing his appearance with Elijah on the mount of Transfiguration as an association with that prophet in God's plan of the ages. They also point to the similarity of many of the plagues of the Time of Jacob's Trouble to those brought by Moses in the deliverance of Israel from Egypt.

These two witnesses will be miraculously protected for "a thousand two hundred and threescore days" (forty-two prophetic months of thirty days each). Their power to bring plagues will draw the attention of the world to their ministry and message: *"These have power to shut heaven, that it rain not in the days of their prophecy: and have power over waters to turn them to blood, and to smite the earth with all plagues, as often as they will"* (Revelation 11:6).

They will undoubtedly herald the countdown of the Tribulation timetable, pointing to the time of the Lord's return to set up His kingdom. It seems likely that many of the Old Testament prophecies concerning the kingdom of Christ will be repeated by these men of God. Perhaps they will cry that the great stone of Daniel's vision is about to fall from heaven, bringing the downfall of all earthly rule and establishing the millennium kingdom (Daniel 2:44, 45).

When the two witnesses have concluded their work they will be slain, and television cameras will beam the sight of their dead bodies lying in the street of Jerusalem to the entire world. The news of their death will cause a celebration among the ungodly of all nations: *"And they that dwell upon the earth shall rejoice over them, and make merry, and shall send gifts one to another; because these two prophets tormented them that dwelt on the earth"* (Revelation 11:10).

After three and a half days they will be resurrected and will ascend to heaven in a cloud while their enemies watch, paralyzed with fear.

5. The Call to Armageddon

The world dictator and his associates will have seen and heard enough. Furious over the success of the 144,000 evangelists and bitter because many Jews have rejected his rule and have turned to Jesus Christ, this dictator will announce a campaign to destroy the Jewish race once and for all. He will blame them for every ill on earth. Every problem in his kingdom will be laid at their door. Every wrong on earth, economic and political, will be charged to them. The hatred and animosity of all the Hamans and Hitlers of history will culminate in this end-time evil ruler.

Having been warned of the time when Christ will return to set up His kingdom, the Antichrist will summon the armies of the earth to the Middle East to destroy the Jews and defeat their Messiah at His coming.

Demonic power will be unleashed.

Miracles performed through satanic power will convince the leaders of the earth who are subservient to the Antichrist to move all their military might to the Middle East to do battle with Christ at His return to the mount of Olives (Zechariah 14:4). *"For they are the spirits of devils, working miracles, which go forth unto the kings of the earth and of the whole world, to gather them to the battle of that great day of God almighty"* (Revelation 16:14).

Joel's ancient prophecy of the greatest military effort of all time will be fulfilled:

> *"Proclaim ye this among the Gentiles; Prepare war, wake up the mighty men, let all the men of war draw near; let them come up: Beat your plowshares into swords, and your pruninghooks into spears: let the weak say, I am strong. Assemble yourselves, and come, all ye heathen, and gather yourselves together round about: thither cause thy mighty ones to come down, O Lord. Let the heathen be wakened, and come up to the valley of Jehoshaphat: for there will I sit to judge all the heathen round about. Put ye in the sickle, for the harvest is ripe: come, get you down; for the press is full, the vats overflow; for their wickedness is great. Multitudes, multitudes in the valley of decision: for the day of the Lord is near in the valley of decision"* (Joel 3:9-14).

Armageddon will demonstrate man at the height of his pride and folly. Convinced of the power of their weaponry and deceived by a leader energized by Satan, the armies of earth will march to their doom, expecting to destroy the Christ they have rejected.

Does this appear to be madness? It did to the psalmist who looked through the centuries and saw it unfold in prophetic vision. He asked: "*Why do the heathen rage, and the people imagine a vain thing?*" (Psalm 2:1).

Explaining the reason for his question, he wrote: "*The kings of the earth set themselves, and the rulers take counsel together, against the LORD, and against his anointed, saying, Let us break their bands asunder, and cast away their cords from us*" (Psalm 2:2,3).

Here is the rebellion of man at its logical end.

And Armageddon will end the rebellion of man.

6. The King Is Coming

Tribulation chronology will have allowed the Antichrist and others to know the time of the return of Christ. The armies of earth under the direction of the Antichrist will have gathered to destroy the Jews and to battle the Lord Himself. Armageddon will have arrived: "*And he gathered them together into a place called in the Hebrew tongue Armageddon*" (Revelation 16:16).

The enemies of the Lord will not be disappointed: Christ will come.

"And I saw heaven opened, and behold a white horse; and he that sat on him was called Faithful and True, and in righteousness he doth judge and make war. His eyes were as a flame of fire, and on his head were many crowns; and he had a name written, that no man knew, but he himself. And he was clothed with a vesture dipped in blood: and his name is called The Word of God. And the armies which were in heaven followed

143

him upon white horses, clothed in fine linen, white and clean. And out of his mouth goeth a sharp sword, that with it he should smite the nations: and he shall rule them with a rod of iron: and he treadeth the winepress of the fierceness and wrath of Almighty God. And he hath on his vesture and on his thigh a name written, KING OF KINGS, AND LORD OF LORDS" (Revelation 19:11-16).

At Armageddon, the most awesome array of deadly weapons ever assembled will be waiting to destroy the returning Christ. In effect, the world's end-time inhabitants will echo the cry of those who rejected the Savior at His first coming: *"We will not have this man to reign over us"* (Luke 19:14).

But the enemies of the Lord will be defeated:

"And I saw the beast, and the kings of the earth, and their armies, gathered together to make war against him that sat on the horse, and against his army. And the beast was taken, and with him the false prophet that wrought miracles before him, with which he deceived them that had received the mark of the beast, and them that worshipped his image. These both were cast alive into a lake of fire burning with brimstone. And the remnant were slain with the sword of him that sat upon the horse, which sword proceeded out of his mouth: and all the fowls were filled with their flesh" (Revelation 19:19-21).

In the wake of the destruction of Armageddon there will be work to do. The church, having returned with the King, will share in these responsibilities. The kingdom of Christ will be established, and the violent drama of the ages will end. There will be peace at last.

14
PEACE AT LAST

Peace will come to Israel and to the world. But it will not come through military might nor treaties produced by the greatest minds on earth. Man's best efforts will ultimately fail, plunging the world into carnage and destruction. Christ will come bringing peace.

When the governments of earth have finally fallen, the Messiah of Israel, the Savior of men, will set up His kingdom (Daniel 2:44).

Upon ending the Battle of Armageddon, Christ the King will judge the nations and destroy the wicked (Matthew 25:31-46). The Beast (the Antichrist) and the False Prophet will be cast into a lake of fire (Revelation 19:20). Satan will be bound for a thousand years (Revelation 20:1-3). And the long-awaited Millennium will begin.

Millennium means one thousand years and refers to the kingdom of Christ on earth. This era, foretold by all the prophets, will be a time of peace among people and nations. War will be but a relic of the painful past. Jerusalem, known for war, bloodshed, and international tensions, will at last become the city of peace and the capital of the world:

> *"And it shall come to pass in the last days, that the mountain of the Lord's house shall be established in the top of the mountains, and shall be exalted above the hills; and all nations shall flow unto it. And many people shall go and say, Come ye, and let us*

go up to the mountain of the LORD, to the house of the God of Jacob; and he will teach us of his ways, and we will walk in his paths: for out of Zion shall go forth the law, and the word of the Lord from Jerusalem. And he shall judge among the nations, and shall rebuke many people: and they shall beat their swords into plowshares, and their spears into pruninghooks; nation shall not lift up sword against nation, neither shall they learn war any more" (Isaiah 2:2-4).

The Prince of Peace will rule from David's throne, and the promises given to Mary concerning Jesus will be fulfilled: *"He shall be great, and shall be called the Son of the Highest: and the Lord God shall give unto him the throne of his father David: And he shall reign over the house of Jacob for ever; and of his kingdom there shall be no end"* (Luke 1:32, 33).

For centuries, the name of Jesus has been feared, hated, or ignored by the Jews. Mistaken people have persecuted them in that name.

Dr. H. A. Ironside once took his umbrella to a Jewish handyman to be repaired. He watched the old man as he worked and was moved by his obvious poverty. When asked the charge the handyman replied, "Thirty-five cents."

Dr. Ironside gave him the thirty-five cents and then said, "I can imagine you have to do many jobs like this to earn a living. Here is an extra half-dollar which I would like to give you in the name of the Lord Jesus Christ."

The old Jew was stunned. He replied, "In the name of Jesus Christ they burned my house in Russia! In the name of Jesus Christ they robbed me of all I had! In the name of Jesus Christ they drove me and my family out into the snow! I have been in America four years, and now for the first time someone speaks to me in the name of Jesus Christ and gives me more money than I ask!" [1]

In the coming age of peace, Jews will love the name of Jesus and will be thrilled with the benefits of His kingdom. Isaiah saw it all more than seven hundred years before the birth of Christ and described their expressions of praise:

"For unto us a child is born, unto us a son is given: and the government shall be upon his shoulder: and his name shall be called Wonderful, Counselor, The mighty God, The everlasting Father, The Prince of Peace. Of the increase of His government and peace there shall be no end, upon the throne of David, and upon his kingdom, to order it, and to establish it with judgment and with justice from henceforth even for ever. The zeal of the LORD of hosts will perform this" (Isaiah. 9:6, 7).

Today Israel walks a tightrope, continually under the threat of invasion by her Arab neighbors. Efforts at peace take a few steps forward, only to retreat as a result of terrorism and bitter hatred by extremists. The Camp David summit meeting, arranged by President Jimmy Carter for Anwar Sadat of Egypt and Menachem Begin of Israel in the fall of 1978, was one such peace-making effort. More will follow involving other nations.

Hopes rise and fall with the temperature of tranquility in the Middle East. But there is a better day coming: *"In that day shall Israel be the third with Egypt and with Assyria, even a blessing in the midst of the land: Whom the Lord of hosts shall bless, saying, Blessed be Egypt my people, and Assyria the work of my hands, and Israel mine inheritance"* (Isaiah 19:24,25).

Peace in the World of Nature

The Millennium will bring peace in the world of nature. All of God's creation suffers as a result of the fall of man and will not be restored until the kingdom of Christ is established on earth:

"For the creature was made subject to vanity, not willingly, but by reason of him who hath subjected the same in hope, Because

147

the creature itself also shall be delivered from the bondage of corruption into the glorious liberty of the children of God. For we know that the whole creation groaneth and travaileth in pain together until now. And not only they, but ourselves also, which have the firstfruits of the Spirit, even we ourselves groan within ourselves, waiting for the adoption, to wit, the redemption of our body" (Romans 8:20-23).

Earthquakes, tornados, floods, and other marks of travail will be absent in the kingdom. Harsh climate changes will be forever past. Nature will cooperate with man.

Productivity will return to the earth. When the Jews returned to their land, they found a desert, and through backbreaking labor and scientific farming they transformed it into a garden. Irrigation made the desert come alive. Citrus orchards replaced arid land denuded of topsoil. Israel became the agricultural showplace of the Middle East.

But Tribulation events will change all that. Plagues and judgments will pummel the earth, and the massive movement of military equipment to the Middle East for the Battle of Armageddon, followed by the awful conflict itself, will finish the destruction. The land will return to rubble again.

Then the King will restore all things:

"The wilderness and the solitary place shall be glad for them; and the desert shall rejoice, and blossom as the rose. It shall blossom abundantly, and rejoice even with joy and singing.... And the parched ground shall become a pool, and the thirsty land springs of water: in the habitation of dragons, where each lay, shall be grass with reeds and rushes" (Isaiah 35:1, 2, 7).

The curse will be removed and harvests will be Edenic:

"Behold, the days come, saith the Lord, that the plowman man shall overtake the reaper, and the treader of grapes him that

148

soweth seed; and the mountains shall drop sweet wine, and all the hills shall melt" (Amos 9:13).

"For the seed shall be prosperous; the vine shall give her fruit, and the ground shall give her increase, and the heavens shall give their dew; and I will cause the remnant of this people to possess all these things" (Zechariah 8:12).

Peace in the Animal World

Even the animal world will be at peace with man. Both Jews and Christians knew the terrifying experience of fighting lions to entertain the Romans. During the reign of the Prince of Peace, the enmity between men and animals will be removed, creating conditions similar to those that prevailed before the Fall:

"The wolf also shall dwell with the lamb, and the leopard shall lie down with the kid; and the calf and the young lion and the fatling together; and a little child shall lead them. And the cow and the bear shall feed; their young ones shall lie down together: and the lion shall eat straw like the ox. And the sucking child shall play on the hole of the asp, and the weaned child shall put his hand on the cockatrice' den" (Isaiah 11:6-8).

Economic Peace

The Millennium will bring economic peace. Because of their business ability, the Jews have been the scapegoat for the economic ills of many nations. Their success has given birth to envy and their skill in handling money has often brought them grief. Hitler's excuse for the holocaust was in large part the claim that the Jews had monopolized the wealth of Germany. Few have recognized Jewish prosperity as the fulfillment of God's promise to Abraham as recorded in Genesis 12:1-3.

The kingdom of Christ will sweep away all economic conflict and will provide fair and enjoyable working conditions. Strikes by workers and oppression by employers will be unknown. Food will be plentiful and there will be sufficient housing for all:

"And they shall build houses, and inhabit them; and they shall plant vineyards, and eat the fruit of them. They shall not build, and another inhabit; they shall not plant, and another eat: for as the days of a tree are the days of my people, and mine elect shall long enjoy the work of their hands. They shall not labour in vain, nor bring forth for trouble; for they are the seed of the blessed of the LORD, and their offspring with them" (Isaiah 65:21-23).

There will be religious peace during the Millennium. The depravity of man is demonstrated in his countless cults and fighting factions among those who claim to be the people of God. Jewish blood flowed in the Rhine Valley from the swords of zealous Crusaders who thought their killing was in the will of God. The Spanish Inquisition preyed on both Jews and Christians in the name of the church. Religious persecution has come from religious rulers as often as from atheists in power.

The kingdom of Christ will find Jews and Gentiles worshipping the Lord together. There will be no mistake about the identity of the Messiah and Savior. He will be known as the King of Kings and Lord of Lords, and all people will praise and honor Him:

"They shall not hurt nor destroy in all my holy mountain: for the earth shall be full of the knowledge of the LORD, as the waters cover the sea. And in that day there shall be a root of Jesse, which shall stand for an ensign of the people; to it shall the Gentiles seek: and his rest shall be glorious" (Isaiah 11:9,10).

"And in that day shall ye say, Praise the Lord, call upon his

name, declare his doings among the people, make mention that his name is exalted" (Isaiah 12:4).

The Jews will experience peace with God in the coming kingdom. Scattered and chastised for generations, these troubled people have wandered and wept, not knowing that peace with God lay but a step of faith away. Their brother Paul had written: *"Therefore being justified by faith, we have peace with God through our Lord Jesus Christ"* (Romans 5:1). He longed for them to know the peace he had found in Christ. Most missed it then, but there is a Jewish revival in the future:

> *"For I will take you from among the heathen, and gather you out of all countries, and will bring you into your own land. Then will I sprinkle clean water upon you, and ye shall be clean: from all your filthiness, and from all your idols, will I cleanse you. A new heart also will I give you, and a new spirit will I put within you: and I will take away the stony heart out of your flesh, and I will give you an heart of flesh. And I will put my spirit within you, and cause you to walk in my statutes, and ye shall keep my judgments, and do them"* (Ezekiel 36:24-27).

Peace in Their Own Land

Finally, in Christ's coming kingdom, the Jews will be at peace in their own land. It will have been a long journey. The promise of this Jewish homeland was first given to Abraham (Genesis 12:1-3), and it has echoed through the centuries. Sometimes the Jews have embraced it and possessed their land. Heroes like Moses, Joshua, and David each had their day in approaching, conquering, or ruling that promised property. Too often their descendents have been disobedient and have suffered defeat and captivity as a result.

The return of the Jews to their land was painful and full of dangers. Their survival in the face of almost certain annihilation must be called miraculous.

Hungry for peace and security, they will make an agreement with the treacherous final world dictator, the Antichrist that will promise protection and tranquility. The treaty will be broken after three and one-half years. And the forty-two months that follow will decimate their land, destroying the fruit of their long labors.

Still, peace will come to Israel. The promise of the prophets will be fulfilled. The Jews will yet dwell in peace in the land of their fathers:

> *"And ye shall dwell in the land that I gave to your fathers; and ye shall be my people, and I will be your God"* (Ezekiel 36:28).

> *"And I will plant them upon their land, and they shall no more be pulled up out of their land which I have given them, saith the Lord thy God"* (Amos 9:15).

Apart from prophetic revelation, one might doubt that lasting peace in the Middle East will ever be more than a Jewish dream. But the Bible is clear: Although born in war and beset by continued threats of destruction, Israel is bound for peace.

When?

When Christ rules there as King. He is the source of peace in any life or land, and He is the One to know and trust in these perplexing hours of closing time.

AFTERWORD:

HOW TO FIND PEACE WITH GOD

The Jews have waited long for peace in their land, and it will come to Israel. But a greater peace is promised by the prophets—individual peace with God.

Isaiah wrote of that peace in his prophecy of the death of Christ: "But he was wounded for our transgressions, he was bruised for our iniquities: the chastisement of our peace was upon him; and with his stripes we are healed" (Isa. 53:5).

People lack peace with God because sin separates them from Him. In recognition of this, for centuries Jews offered animal sacrifices to atone for their sins. Each sacrifice looked forward to the day when all sins would be paid for by the coming Savior: "All we like sheep have gone astray; we have turned every one to his own way; and the LORD hath laid on him the iniquity of us all" (Isa. 53:6).

John the Baptist said of Jesus: ". . . Behold the Lamb of God, which taketh away the sin of the world" (John 1:29).

Now full payment for sin has been made. The death of Christ on the cross fulfilled all the righteous demands of the law. Forgiveness for sin is available: ". . . the blood of Jesus Christ his Son cleanseth us from all sin" (1 John 1:7).

Do you want to have peace with God? It can be yours through faith in Jesus Christ: "Therefore being justified by faith, we have peace with God through our Lord Jesus Christ" (Rom. 5:1).

To take Jesus Christ by faith is to turn from your sin (repent) and place all trust (confidence, belief) in Him as your personal

153

Savior and Lord.

Now it is time to act on this truth. Here is a prayer to guide you:

> *"Dear Lord Jesus, I come to you just as I am, a sinner. I turn from my sin to you. I now take you by faith as my own Savior and Lord. I trust you to save me and guide me in the Christian life.*
> *In your name, amen!"*

Repeating a prayer does not bring peace with God. But heartfelt faith in Christ does: *"With the heart man believeth unto righteousness; and with the mouth confession is made unto salvation"* (Rom. 10:10).

Think carefully about the words of the prayer above. Are they an expression of genuine faith in your heart?

If so, you now have peace with God.

Thank Him for His peace and salvation.

APPENDIX:

THE DECLARATION OF INDEPENDENCE OF THE STATE OF ISRAEL

Issued at Tel Aviv on May 14,1948

The Land of Israel was the birthplace of the Jewish people. Here their spiritual, religious, and national identity was formed. Here they achieved independence and created a culture of national and universal significance. Here they wrote and gave the Bible to the world.

Exiled from Palestine, the Jewish people remained faithful to it in all the countries of their dispersion, never ceasing to pray and hope for their return and the restoration of their national freedom.

Impelled by this historic association, Jews strove throughout the centuries to go back to the land of their fathers and regain their statehood. In recent decades they returned in masses. They reclaimed the wilderness, revived their language, built cities and villages and established a vigorous and ever-growing community with its own economic and cultural life. They sought peace yet were ever prepared to defend themselves. They brought the blessing of progress to all inhabitants of the country.

In the year 1897 the First Zionist Congress, inspired by Theodor Herzl's vision of the Jewish State, proclaimed the right of the Jewish people to national revival in their own country.

This right was acknowledged by the Balfour Declaration of November 2, 1917, and reaffirmed by the Mandate of the League of Nations, which gave explicit international recognition to the historic connection of the Jewish people with Palestine and their right to reconstitute their National Home.

The Nazi holocaust, which engulfed millions of Jews in Europe, proved anew the urgency of the re-establishment of the Jewish State, which would solve the problem of Jewish homelessness by opening the gates to all Jews and lifting the Jewish people to equality in the family of nations.

The survivors of the European catastrophe, as well as Jews from other lands, proclaiming their right to a life of dignity, freedom, and labor, and undeterred by hazards, hardships, and obstacles, have tried unceasingly to enter Palestine.

In the Second World War the Jewish people in Palestine made a full contribution in the struggle of the freedom-loving nations against the Nazi evil. The sacrifices of their soldiers and the efforts of their workers gained them title to rank with the peoples who founded the United Nations.

On November 29, 1947, the General Assembly of the United Nations adopted a Resolution for the establishment of an independent Jewish State in Palestine, and called upon the inhabitants of the country to take such steps as may be necessary on their part to put the plan into effect.

This recognition by the United Nations of the right of the Jewish people to establish their independent State may not be revoked. It is moreover, the self-evident right of the Jewish people to be a nation, as all other nations, in its own sovereign State.

ACCORDINGLY, WE, the members of the National Council, representing the Jewish people in Palestine and the Zionist movement of the world, met together in solemn assembly today, the day of termination of the British Mandate for Palestine, by virtue of the national and historic right of the Jewish people and of the Resolution of the General Assembly of the United Nations,

HEREBY PROCLAIM the establishment of the Jewish State in Palestine, to be called ISRAEL.

WE HEREBY DECLARE that as from the termination of the Mandate at midnight, this night of the 14th to 15th May, 1948, and until the setting up of the duly elected bodies of the State in accordance with a Constitution, to be drawn up by a Constituent Assembly not later than the first day of October, 1948, the present National Council shall act as the provisional administration, shall constitute the Provisional Government of the State of Israel.

THE STATE OF ISRAEL will be open to the immigration of Jews from all countries of their dispersion; will promote the development of the country for the benefit of all its inhabitants; will be based on the precepts of liberty, justice, and peace taught by the Hebrew Prophets; will uphold the full social and political equality of all its citizens, without distinction of race, creed, or sex; will guarantee full freedom of conscience, worship, education, and culture; will safeguard the sanctity and inviolability of the shrines and Holy Places of all religions; and will dedicate itself to the principles of the Charter of the United Nations.

THE STATE OF ISRAEL will be ready to cooperate with the organs and representatives of the United Nations in the implementation of the Resolution of the Assembly of November 29, 1947, and will take steps to bring about an Economic Union over the whole of Palestine.

We appeal to the United Nations to assist the Jewish people in the building of its State and to admit Israel into the family of nations.

In the midst of wanton aggression, we yet call upon Arab inhabitants of the State of Israel to return to the ways of peace and play their part in the development of the State, with full and equal citizenship and due representation in all its bodies and institutions—provisional or permanent.

We offer peace and amity to all neighboring states and their peoples, and invite them to cooperate with the independent Jewish nation for the common good of all.

Our call goes out to the Jewish people all over the world to rally to our side in the task of immigration and development of the dream of generations—the redemption of Israel.

With trust in Almighty God, we set our hand to this Declaration, at this Session of the Provisional State Council, in the city of Tel Aviv, on this Sabbath eve, the fifth of Iyar, 5708, the fourteenth of May, 1948.

NOTES

Chapter 1

1. Walter B. Knight, *Knights Treasury of Illustrations* (Grand Rapids: Wm. B. Eerdmans, 1963), p. 349.

2. Walter B. Knight, *Three Thousand Illustrations for Christian Service* (Grand Rapids: Wm. B. Eerdmans, 1947), p. 717.

3. Douglas MacArthur, *Reminiscences* (New York: McGraw-Hill, 1964), p.404.

4. Dr. David Bradley, *No Place to Hide* (Boston: Little, Brown, & Co., 1948), p. 88.

5. Quoted in Charles Pont, *The World's Collision* (Boston: W.A. Wilde, 1956), p. 85.

Chapter 2

1. H. A. Ironside, *Daniel the Prophet* (Neptune, N.J.: Loizeaux Brothers, 1911), p. 25.

2. Alva J. McClain, *Daniel's Prophecy of the Seventy Weeks* (Grand Rapids: Zondervan, 1940), p. 5.

Chapter 3

1. *Scofield Reference Bible* (New York: Oxford Univ. Press, 1967).

Chapter 4

1. Dr. Charles Pont, *The World's Collision* (Boston: W. A. Wilde Co., 1956), pp. 102, 107.

Chapter 6

1. Knight, *Three Thousand Illustrations,* p. 385.

2. Mark Twain, *The Innocents Abroad* (New York: Harper and Brothers, 1869).

3. *Near East Report* 18:6 (February 6, 1974), p. 6.

4. Walter B. Knight, *Knight's Master Book of Illustrations* (Grand Rapids: Wm. B. Eerdmans, 1956), p. 340.

5. Maurice Samuel, *Light on Israel* (New York: Alfred A. Knopf, 1968), p. 84.

Chapter 7

1. Knight, *Treasury of Illustrations, p.* 188.

2. Samuel, *Light on Israel,* pp. 77-78.

3. Arthur D. Morse, *While Six Million Died* (New York: Random House, 1967), p. 105.

4. *Ibid.,* p. 114.

5. Quoted in Joe Bayly, "Good Samaritans' Stain," *Eternity* (July 1978). Originally appeared in a *Manchester Guardian* article by Peggy Mann entitled "When the World Passed by on the Other Side."

6. *Ibid.*

7. *Ibid.*

8. *Ibid.*

9. *Ibid.*

10. Jacob Presser, *The Destruction of the Dutch Jews* (New

York: E. P. Dutton, 1969), p. 456.

11. *Ibid.*,p.486.

12. Presser, *Dutch Jews,* p. 336.

13. Pont, *World's Collision,* p. 279.

14. *Ibid.,* p. 102.

Chapter 8

1. David M. Jacobs and Kees Scherer, *Israel* (Chicago: Follett, 1968), p. 31.

2. *New York Times,* May 14, 1948.

3. William L. Hull, *Israel, the Key to Prophecy* (Grand Rapids: Zondervan, 1957), p. 22.

Chapter 9

1. *Near East Report* 18:6 (February 6, 1974).

2. *Ibid.*

3. *Ibid.*

4. *Ibid.*

Chapter 10

1. Walvoord and Walvoord, *Armageddon,* pp. 113-14.

Chapter 11

1. H. A. Ironside, *Lectures on the Revelation* (Neptune, N.J.: Loizeaux Brothers, 1919), p. 103.

Chapter 12

1. H. A. Ironside, *Ezekiel* (Neptune, N.J.: Loizeaux Brothers, 1949), p. 267.

2. *Scofield Reference Bible.*

3. Pont, *World's Collision,* p. 212.

4. *Scofield Reference Bible.*

Chapter 13

1. Milton Lindberg, *The Jews and Armageddon* (Chicago: American Messianic Fellowship, 1940), p. 24.

2. *Ibid.*, p. 26.

Chapter 14

1. Knight, *Master Book of Illustrations,* p. 336.

INDEX

163

King Boleslav the Pious, 50
King John, 52
Kingdom of Christ, 23, 26, 28, 29,
    106, 11, 113, 117, 137, 139-
    141, 144-151
Knight, Walter Brown, 56
Koller, Carl, 74
Kuwait, 99

Lapierre, Dominique, 62
Latter Days, 9, 25, 130
Latter Years, 107, 128, 130
Lebanon, 93, 99
Libya, 125, 128
Lindberg, Milton B., 138
Lindbergh, Charles, 21
Little Horn, 34, 121
Lord Peel, 74
Lowth, Robert, 127
Luke, 21, 35, 36, 38, 39, 43, 100,
    144, 146

MacArthur, General Douglas,
    14, 15
McClain, Alva J., 30
Magog, 124-128
Maimonides, Moses, 48
Mark of the Beast, 10, 118, 120,
    144
Marriage Supper of the Lamb,
    112
Mary, 36-38, 146
Mauthausen, 80
Medo-Persian, 26, 28
Meshech, 124-127
Micah, 37, 38, 106

Millennium, 10, 112, 145, 147,
    149, 150
Minkowsky, 74
Moses, 43, 46, 47, 49, 53, 79, 80,
    103, 120, 140, 141, 151
Mount of Megiddo, 134

Napoleon, 22, 137
Nasser, Gamel Abdel, 98-100, 104
Nebuchadnezzar, 23-29, 46, 53
Nehemiah, 31, 32, 89
Nero, 44
Newton, Sir Isaac, 20
North Africa, 48
North Pole, 17

Paul, 19, 42, 109, 112, 113, 139,
    151
Persia, 124, 125
Pestilences, 16, 17, 132
Peter, 42
Peter the Great, 126
Pettingill, Dr. William, 41
Phut, 124
Pilate, 42
Poland, 50, 52, 80
Pont, Dr. Charles E., 53

Queen Victoria, 55

Rapture, 10, 33, 111-113, 122
Red Horse, 119
Rhine Valley, 48, 50, 52, 104, 150
Roman Empire, 22, 26, 28, 33, 34,
    37, 84, 121, 131
Rosh, 127